Pub & Inns of Britain

11

- Including Family-friendly & Dog-friendly Pubs
- Accommodation, food and traditional good cheer

Battlesteads Country Hotel & Restaurant, Hexham, Northumberland (page 109)

Foreword

Since early times there have been inns and taverns to cater for the traveller, and for the working man (and woman) needing refreshment after a hard and gruelling day. Some of these inns and taverns still exist today, along with numerous, more recently built pubs and small hotels, all of which offer the traveller, and the casual or regular visitor, the chance to rest, enjoy good food and drink, and exchange pleasantries with friends and new acquaintances.

In **Pubs & Inns of Britain 2011** you will find a number of such establishments where you can stop for meal or a drink, or even for a longer stay. Refer to our Pet Friendly or Family Friendly Supplements starting on page 170 if you are travelling with children or pets, or use our Readers' Offer Vouchers on pages 179 to save money on family outings.

© FHG Guides Ltd, 2011
ISBN 978-1-85055-432-5

Maps: ©MAPS IN MINUTES™ / Collins Bartholomew (2009)

Typeset by FHG Guides Ltd, Paisley.
Printed and bound in China by Imago.

Distribution. Book Trade: ORCA Book Services, Stanley House,
3 Fleets Lane, Poole, Dorset BH15 3AJ
(Tel: 01202 665432; Fax: 01202 666219)
e-mail: mail@orcabookservices.co.uk
Published by FHG Guides Ltd., Abbey Mill Business Centre,
Seedhill, Paisley PA1 1TJ (Tel: 0141-887 0428; Fax: 0141-889 7204).
e-mail: admin@fhguides.co.uk

Pubs & Inns of Britain is published by FHG Guides Ltd,
part of Kuperard Group.

Cover design: FHG Guides
Cover Picture:
Fisherman's Haunt Inn, Christchurch, Dorset, courtesy of Fullers Inns.
(full details on Outside Back Cover)

Contents

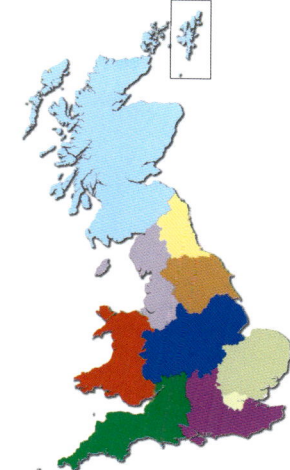

Foreword	2
Pet Friendly Pubs	170
Family Friendly Pubs	177
Readers' Offer Vouchers	179
Index	205

SOUTH WEST ENGLAND — 5
Cornwall, Devon, Dorset, Gloucestershire, Somerset, Wiltshire

LONDON & SOUTH EAST ENGLAND — 36
London (Central & Greater), Berkshire, Buckinghamshire, Hampshire, Isle of Wight, Kent, Oxfordshire, Surrey, East Sussex, West Sussex

EAST OF ENGLAND — 64
Bedfordshire, Cambridgeshire, Essex, Hertfordshire, Norfolk, Suffolk

MIDLANDS — 79
Derbyshire, Herefordshire, Leicestershire & Rutland, Northamptonshire, Nottinghamshire, Shropshire, Warwickshire, Worcestershire

YORKSHIRE — 94
East Yorkshire, North Yorkshire,

NORTH EAST ENGLAND — 106
Northumberland, Tyne & Wear

NORTH WEST ENGLAND — 114
Cheshire, Cumbria, Lancashire, Greater Manchester

SCOTLAND

Aberdeen, Banff & Moray	137
Argyll & Bute	140
Borders	144
Edinburgh & Lothians	145
Fife	147
Highlands	148
Perth & Kinross	151
Stirling & The Trossachs	153
Scottish Islands	154

WALES

Anglesey & Gwynedd	158
North Wales	159
Carmarthenshire	162
Ceredigion	163
Pembrokeshire	164
Powys	166
South Wales	168

IRELAND

Co. Wicklow	169

England and Wales • Counties

1. Plymouth
2. Torbay
3. Poole
4. Bournemouth
5. Southampton
6. Portsmouth
7. Brighton & Hove
8. Medway
9. Thurrock
10. Southend
11. Slough
12. Windsor & Maidenhead
13. Bracknell Forest
14. Wokingham
15. Reading
16. West Berkshire
17. Swindon
18. Bath & Northeast Somerset
19. North Somerset
20. Bristol
21. South Gloucestershire
22. Luton
23. Milton Keynes
24. Peterborough
25. Leicester
26. Nottingham
27. Derby
28. Telford & Wrekin
29. Stoke-on-Trent
30. Warrington
31. Halton
32. Merseyside
33. Blackburn with Darwen
34. Blackpool
35. N.E. Lincolnshire
36. North Lincolnshire
37. Kingston-upon-Hull
38. York
39. Redcar & Cleveland
40. Middlesborough
41. Stockton-on-Tees
42. Darlington
43. Hartlepool

NORTH WALES
a. Denbighshire
b. Flintshire
c. Wrexham

SOUTH WALES
d. Swansea
e. Neath & Port Talbot
f. Bridgend
g. Rhondda Cynon Taff
h. Merthyr Tydfil
i. Vale of Glamorgan
j. Cardiff
k. Caerphilly
l. Blaenau Gwent
m. Torfaen
n. Newport
o. Monmouthshire

SOUTH WEST ENGLAND — Cornwall 5

Cornwall

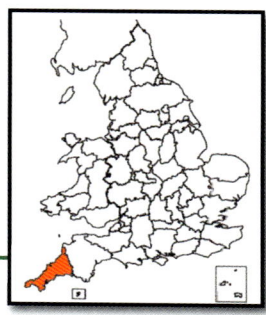

Colliford Tavern — "AN OASIS ON BODMIN MOOR"
Colliford Lake, Near St Neot, Liskeard, Cornwall PL14 6PZ • Tel: 01208 821335
e-mail: info@colliford.com • www.colliford.com

Set in attractive grounds which include a children's play area, ponds and a working waterwheel, this delightfully furnished free house offers good food and bar snacks. Sprucely-appointed guest rooms are spacious and have en suite shower, colour television, radio alarm, beverage maker and numerous thoughtful extras.

An unusual feature of the tavern is a 37' deep granite well. In the midst of the scenic splendour of Bodmin Moor, this is a relaxing country retreat only a few minutes' walk from Colliford Lake, so popular with fly fishermen. Both north and south coasts are within easy driving distance and terms are most reasonable. Adjacent to Colliford Adventure Park - discounted entrance to indoor/outdoor attractions, lake/wood walks and animals.

Campsite for touring caravans, motorhomes and tents - full electric hook-up etc available.

6 BEDROOMS, ALL WITH PRIVATE BATHROOM. FREE HOUSE WITH REAL ALE. CHILDREN WELCOME. BAR SNACKS, RESTAURANT, FUNCTION ROOM. TOTALLY NON-SMOKING. BODMIN 7 MILES. S££, D££.

The Crown Inn
Lanlivery, Near Bodmin, Cornwall PL30 5BT
Tel: 01208 872707 • www.wagtailinns.com

Charming free house, located on the 'Saints Way' in Cornwall and dating back to the 12th century. It has traditional low beams, open fires, and an inviting restaurant serving meat and fish dishes prepared daily from local produce. The inn is an ideal base for sightseeing in and around this Cornish area of natural beauty.

BULLERS ARMS HOTEL
Marhamchurch, Bude, EX23 0HB
Freehouse - Est Circa 1856

- Hunters Bar - all homemade fayre lunchtime and evening dining with daily specials
- Sunday Carvery - with a choice of 4 meats and 7 vegetables
- En - suite Accommodation - with a hearty full English breakfast
- Cask Marque accredited real ales
- Functions, Banquets, Parties
- Licensed to conduct civil ceremonies
- Business conferences, meetings (LCD projector, PA etc. available)

☎ 01288 361277

www.bullersarms.co.uk
enquiries@bullersarms.co.uk

ALL BEDROOMS WITH PRIVATE BATHROOM. FREE HOUSE WITH REAL ALE.
CHILDREN AND PETS WELCOME. BAR AND RESTAURANT MEALS.
LAUNCESTON 15 MILES.

The Springer Spaniel
Treburley, near Launceston, Cornwall PL15 9NS
Tel: 01579 370424
enquiries@thespringerspaniel.org.uk
www.thespringerspaniel.org.uk

Relax in the friendly and informal atmosphere.
The perfect place for a casual drink, family lunch
or a venue for a celebration.
Specialising in home cooked, fresh, locally sourced food.
Emphasis upon game, with beef and lamb from the
owner's organic farm.

NO ACCOMMODATION. REAL ALE.
CHILDREN AND PETS WELCOME. BAR AND RESTAURANT MEALS. DESIGNATED COVERED SMOKING AREA.
CALLINGTON 5 MILES.

OLD FERRY INN (on facing page)

12 BEDROOMS, ALL WITH PRIVATE BATHROOM. ALL BEDROOMS NON-SMOKING. REAL ALE.
PETS WELCOME. BAR MEALS, RESTAURANT EVENINGS ONLY.
ST AUSTELL 9 MILES. D£/££.

Why not come for a well deserved holiday to the family-run Old Ferry Inn, close to the edge of the beautiful River Fowey. There are many varied walks from country and riverside to breathtaking views along the Cornwall Coastal Path. The 400-year-old hotel has an excellent à la carte restaurant for evening meals and a comprehensive bar menu for lunch and evening. The Inn has 12 letting rooms with tea and coffee making facilities, colour TV and telephone. All rooms have en suite or private facilities, and most have river views.

The Old Ferry Inn

Bodinnick-by-Fowey PL23 1LX
Tel: (01726) 870237 • Fax: (01726) 870116
www.oldferryinn.com • e-mail: royce972@aol.com

Prices are from £90-£130 per night for two people sharing

Cornwall — SOUTH WEST ENGLAND

Mount View Hotel

The Mount View is a detached Victorian hotel, built in 1894. This family-run public house is situated approximately 100 yards from the Mounts Bay beach, which runs between Penzance and Marazion.

There is an extensive menu including vegetarian choices, and the bar offers a good selection of wine, beer and spirits.

There are five letting rooms, three en suite, all with colour TV and tea/coffee making.

Dogs are welcome but they must be well behaved, and sociable with other dogs, and people.

Private parking • Open all year.

Longrock, Penzance, Cornwall TR20 8JJ
Tel: 01736 710416

We are situated between Penzance and Marazion, approx. one mile from each, and half a mile from the heliport which provides an air link to the Isles of Scilly. The hotel is ideally situated to explore West Cornwall, with easy access to St Michaels Mount, St Ives, and Lands End. There are a number of easily accessible golf courses, sea and coarse fishing venues, and we are 100 yards from the South West Coastal Path. The local scuba diving centre is a short drive away, and nature lovers will find the nearby RSPB reserve at Marazion Marshes well worth a visit.

5 BEDROOMS, 3 WITH PRIVATE BATHROOM.
CHILDREN AND PETS WELCOME. BAR MEALS.
TRURO 24 MILES. S£, D££/£££.

THE RISING SUN INN
Altarnun, Launceston, Cornwall PL15 7SN • Tel: 01566 86636
www.therisingsuninn.co.uk

The Rising Sun is a country pub and has retained many features from its origins as a 16th century inn. It is the ideal place to escape to for a pint of your favourite ale, a game of dart or pool - and don't miss the home-cooked burgers, lasagne, fish dishes and meat pies.

Cornwall, with the longest stretch of coastline in the UK, has become a major centre for watersports, whether sailing, surfing, windsurfing, water-skiing, diving in the clear waters to explore historic wrecks or enjoying a family beach holiday. There are busy fishing towns like Looe, Padstow, and traditional villages such as Polperro, with plenty of inns and restaurants where you can sample the fresh catch. There are gardens at Mount Edgcumbe and the Lost Garden of Heligan, as well as a wide choice of National Trust properties including Lanhydrock. The magnificent coast is ideal for birdwatchers, artists and photographers, while Bodmin Moor, one of Cornwall's 12 Areas of Outstanding Natural Beauty, is well worth a visit.

SOUTH WEST ENGLAND — Cornwall

The Godolphin Arms

West End, Marazion, Cornwall TR17 0EN

Perched on the edge of the sand, directly opposite St Michael's Mount in historic Marazion, this family-run Inn offers ten en suite guest bedrooms, a choice of bars, beachside terrace and a varied menu. The outlook from the lounge bar and many of the bedrooms is simply stunning, with uninterrupted views to the Island and castle and across Mounts Bay towards Penzance. Perfect for exploring coast and coves.

Highly Commended in Cornwall Tourism Awards 'Pub of the Year'

01736 710202
e-mail: enquiries@godolphinarms.co.uk
www.godolphinarms.co.uk

10 BEDROOMS, ALL WITH PRIVATE BATHROOM. ALL BEDROOMS NON-SMOKING. CHILDREN WELCOME. BAR AND RESTAURANT MEALS. PENZANCE 3 MILES. S£££, D££.

Rates

Normal Bed & Breakfast rate per person (single room)

PRICE RANGE	CATEGORY
Under £35	S£
£36-£45	S££
£46-£55	S£££
Over £55	S££££

Normal Bed & Breakfast rate per person (sharing double/twin room)

PRICE RANGE	CATEGORY
Under £35	D£
£36-£45	D££
£46-£55	D£££
Over £55	D££££

This is meant as an indication only and does not show prices for Special Breaks, Weekends, etc. Guests are therefore advised to verify all prices on enquiring or booking.

This renowned 17th century inn is situated in an unspoilt fishing cove on the rugged North Coast of Cornwall. The beach is just 50 yards from the front door and the Coastal Path offers miles of breathtaking scenery.

For a relaxing break with a friendly atmosphere you need look no further. Golf, fishing, sailing and riding are all nearby.

All our rooms are en suite and centrally heated. We provide colour TV, radio, direct dial telephone, tea-making facilities and a hair dryer.

Pets welcome in the Inn and Self-catering accommodation available.

Port Gaverne Hotel
Near Port Isaac, Cornwall PL29 3SQ
Tel: 01208 880244 • Fax: 01208 880151
www.port-gaverne-hotel.co.uk

Finnygook Inn

Beautiful 15th Century Coaching Inn with 5 en suite bedrooms. The Inn has a cosy bar with open fires and a delightful restaurant/library. We serve fantastic food freshly prepared with all local produce. The Inn has a beer garden, all very private and with panoramic views over the River Tamar.
100 yards away is an 18 hole cliff top golf course and the coastal footpath.
Food is served all day and we have an extensive collection of fine wines and cask ales.
A real delight.

Crafthole, Torpoint, Cornwall PL11 3BQ
Tel: 01503 230338
e-mail: eat@finnygook.co.uk • www.finnygook.co.uk

5 BEDROOMS, ALL WITH PRIVATE BATHROOM. ALL BEDROOMS NON-SMOKING. FREE HOUSE WITH REAL ALE. CHILDREN AND PETS WELCOME. BAR AND RESTAURANT MEALS.
TORPOINT 5 MILES. S££, D££££.

Rates

S – SINGLE ROOM rate   D – Sharing DOUBLE/TWIN ROOM

S£ D£ = Under £35   S££ D££ = £36-£45   S£££ D£££ = £46-£55   S££££ D££££ = Over £55

This is meant as an indication only and does not show prices for Special Breaks, Weekends, etc. Guests are therefore advised to verify all prices on enquiring or booking.

FREE or **REDUCED RATE** entry to Holiday Visits and Attractions – see our **READERS' OFFER VOUCHERS** on pages 179-204

PORT GAVERNE HOTEL (on facing page)

15 BEDROOMS, ALL WITH PRIVATE BATHROOM. ALL BEDROOMS NON-SMOKING. FREE HOUSE WITH REAL ALE. CHILDREN AND PETS WELCOME. BAR AND RESTAURANT MEALS.
WADEBRIDGE 5 MILES. S£££, D£££.

THE New Inn

Veryan, Truro, Cornwall TR2 5QA

Set in a picturesque village on the Roseland Peninsula, the New Inn is a small granite pub, originally consisting of two cottages and was built in the 16th century.

Visitors are welcome to enjoy the atmosphere in our local village bar and we are locally renowned for our good food and cask ales, a wide range of food being served in the bar.

Accommodation consists of spacious and comfortable rooms – one single with separate private facilities, and one double and one twin en suite. St Austell and Truro are nearby, and we are situated close to the beautiful sandy beaches of Pendower and Carne.

AA ★★★★ INN

Tel: 01872 501362 • Fax: 01872 501078 • www.newinnveryan.co.uk

3 BEDROOMS, ALL WITH PRIVATE BATHROOM. ALL BEDROOMS NON-SMOKING.
BAR AND RESTAURANT MEALS.
MEVAGISSEY 7 MILES. ££

Other British holiday guides from FHG Guides

300 GREAT HOTELS
SHORT BREAK HOLIDAYS
The bestselling and original **PETS WELCOME!**
500 GREAT PLACES TO STAY
THE GOLF GUIDE - *Where to Play, Where to Stay*
SELF-CATERING HOLIDAYS • **BED & BREAKFAST STOPS**
CARAVAN & CAMPING HOLIDAYS • **FAMILY BREAKS**

Published annually: available in all good bookshops or direct from the publisher:
FHG Guides, Abbey Mill Business Centre, Seedhill, Paisley PA1 1TJ
Tel: 0141 887 0428 • Fax: 0141 889 7204
e-mail: admin@fhguides.co.uk • www.holidayguides.com

Devon

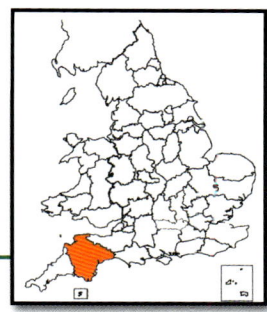

THE HOOPS INN & COUNTRY HOTEL

**Horns Cross, Near Clovelly,
Bideford, Devon EX39 5DL
Tel: 01237 451222 • Fax: 01237 451247
e-mail: sales@hoopsinn.co.uk   www.hoopsinn.co.uk**

This picturebook thatched country inn blends 13th century charm with 21st century luxury and extends a warm welcome to its guests. Relax by one of the open log fires to soak up the olde worlde atmosphere while enjoying a real ale or wine before dining on the best of local fish, game or meat, including house favourites: seafood platters, half shoulder of lamb in onion gravy. Choose from over 200 wines. All bedrooms are en suite, individually furnished and well appointed. The superior rooms under the old thatch have romantic antique canopy beds. AA Red Rosette Restaurant. The Hoops is a splendid base for a combined sea, country or touring holiday, with opportunities for walking, cycling, fishing, golf, together with historic gardens, houses, and the world-famous fishing village of Clovelly on the doorstep, and Dartmoor and Exmoor within easy reach.

13 BEDROOMS, ALL WITH PRIVATE BATHROOM. ALL BEDROOMS NON-SMOKING FREE HOUSE WITH REAL ALE. CHILDREN AND PETS WELCOME. BAR MEALS, RESTAURANT EVENINGS ONLY. DESIGNATED COVERED SMOKING AREA. CLOVELLY 5 MILES. S££££, D£££.

Dartmoor Lodge
**Peartree Cross, Ashburton, Devon TQ13 7JW
Tel: 01364 652232 • 01364 652901 • www.dartmoorlodge.co.uk**

There is no better place for walkers and lovers of wide-open spaces, with the attractions of the National Park on the doorstep. It is positioned equidistant between Plymouth and Exeter, both superb for culture and shopping. Dartmoor Lodge caters for every occasion, with modern facilities in both function suites as well as in the bedrooms.

The Tuckers Arms

Dalwood, Axminster, Devon EX13 7EG

This is a beautiful old English pub with a thatched roof, low beamed ceilings, flagstone floors and inglenook fireplaces. It is situated just off the A35 to the east of Honiton in the heart of Sir Francis Drake country.

The 800-year-old inn, built originally as a hunting lodge for the Duke of Beaulieu, nestles beside the babbling Cory brook, overlooked by Danes Hill, the site of a fort built by the marauding Vikings who came to these parts long before the Norman conquest. But Dalwood has not been invaded by tourists - this is rural England at its best and quietest!

Our rooms are extremely comfortable and have colour TV, tea & coffee making facilities, and en suite power showers.

At the Tucker's Arms we specialise in fresh fish and game; locally caught crab, lobster and lemon sole are regularly featured on our menu. These are supplemented by imaginative starters, and super home-made sweets. Local cheeses and clotted cream feature on the menu at all times.

01404 881342
www.tuckersarms.co.uk
reservations@tuckersarms.co.uk

SOUTH WEST ENGLAND — Devon

THE RED LION INN
Dittisham, Near Dartmouth, Devon TQ6 0ES
www.redliondittisham.co.uk

The Red Lion has been offering generous hospitality since 1750 when it was a Coaching House. Log fires and gleaming brass in a friendly old bar, hearty English breakfasts, terraced gardens overlooking the River Dart, and an exceptionally warm welcome all await you. Bedrooms are individually furnished, with comfortable beds, central heating, colour television, tea-making facilities and telephones. An extensive menu includes daily specials and features fresh produce, prime local meats, fresh fish and locally grown vegetables. Picturesque countryside and a mild climate make this a perfect holiday retreat.

Tel: 01803 722235

6 BEDROOMS, ALL WITH PRIVATE BATHROOM. ALL BEDROOMS NON-SMOKING. FREE HOUSE WITH REAL ALE. BAR MEALS.
DARTMOUTH 5 MILES. S£££, D£££.

Staghunters Inn/Hotel
Brendon, Exmoor EX35 6PS

- Family-run village inn with frontage to the East Lyn river, set in four acres of garden and paddock. This cosy hotel features log fires, fine wines and traditional ales.
- 12 en suite bedrooms with central heating, TV and tea/coffee making facilities.
- Meals are available in the bar and restaurant using fresh local produce; vegetarian dishes served.
- Fishing, shooting and riding available; own stables.
- Ample car parking.
Open all year. Terms on request.

Owners: The Wyburn Family.

e-mail: stay@staghunters.com
www.staghunters.com
Tel: 01598 741222
Fax: 01598 741352

12 BEDROOMS, ALL WITH PRIVATE BATHROOM. REAL ALE.
BAR AND RESTAURANT MEALS.
LYNTON 3 MILES. S£, D£.

THE TUCKERS ARMS (on facing page)

ALL BEDROOMS WITH PRIVATE BATHROOMS. REAL ALE.
RESTAURANT MEALS.
AXMINSTER 3 MILES.

Mark and Judy Harrison welcome you to

THE ROYAL OAK INN
Dunsford, Devon

The Royal Oak is a traditional village pub in the heart of the beautiful Devon village of Dunsford. It's a family-run place with a warm, friendly atmosphere and something for everyone.

Real ales from all over Britain. The kitchen serves generous portions of home-cooked good food with regular well-known specials.

The Royal Oak has a walled courtyard and a large Beer Garden with beautiful views across Dunsford and the Teign Valley

Dogs on leads are welcome and there are lots of animals to visit, great for children with our own play area. Plenty of off-road parking.

Quiet newly refurbished en suite bedrooms are available in the tastefully converted 400 year old granite and cob cob barn located to the rear of the Inn. All non-smoking. Each room has its own front door which opens out onto a pretty, walled courtyard. Ideal base for touring Dartmoor, Exeter and the coast

The Royal Oak Inn
Dunsford, Near Exeter, Devon EX6 7DA

TEL: 01647 252256 • e-mail:mark@troid.co.uk • www.royaloakd.com

The Foxhunters Inn
West Down, Near Ilfracombe EX34 8NU

- 300 year-old coaching Inn conveniently situated for beaches and country walks.
- Serving good local food.
- En suite accommodation.
- Pets allowed in bar areas and beer garden, may stay in accommodation by prior arrangement. Water bowls provided.

Tel: 01271 863757 • Fax: 01271 879313
www.foxhuntersinn.co.uk

8 BEDROOMS, ALL WITH PRIVATE BATHROOM. ALL BEDROOMS NON-SMOKING. CHILDREN AND PETS WELCOME. BAR AND RESTAURANT MEALS.
ILFRACOMBE 4 MILES. S££££, D££.

The Weary Ploughman
Dartmouth Road, Churston Ferrers, Brixham, Devon TQ5 0LL
Tel: 01803 844 702 • www.wearyploughman.co.uk

Originally a railway hotel, this pub/ restaurant/ hotel provides locals and business persons with a relaxing sanctuary in which to eat, drink, and relax. There is a good selection of fine wines and ales in the bar, freshly prepared fare in the restaurant and de luxe accommodation at an affordable price.

The Anchor Inn
Fore Street, Beer, Near Seaton, Devon EX12 3ET
Tel: 01297 203 86 • www.anchorinn-beer.co.uk

Visitors can expect a high standard of hospitality at The Anchor Inn, which has a specialist seafood restaurant and friendly staff. 8 en suite bedrooms provide all modern facilities, each overlooking the unspoilt East Devon fishing village. Why not curl up beside the bar's open log fire in winter or relax in the clifftop beer garden during the summer months?

THE ROYAL OAK INN (on facing page)

5 ROOMS, ALL EN SUITE. REAL ALE.
CHILDREN AND PETS WELCOME. BAR MEALS.
MORETONHAMPSTEAD 4 MILES.

Blue Ball Inn
formerly The Exmoor Sandpiper Inn

is a romantic Coaching Inn dating in part back to the 13th century, with low ceilings, blackened beams, stone fireplaces and a timeless atmosphere of unspoilt old world charm. Offering visitors great food and drink, a warm welcome and a high standard of accommodation.

The inn is set in an imposing position on a hilltop on Exmoor in North Devon, a few hundred yards from the sea, and high above the twin villages of Lynmouth and Lynton, in an area of oustanding beauty.
The spectacular scenery and endless views attract visitors and hikers from all over the world.

We have 16 en suite bedrooms, comfortable sofas in the bar and lounge areas, and five fireplaces, including a 13th century inglenook. Our extensive menus include local produce wherever possible, such as locally reared meat, amd locally caught game and fish, like Lynmouth Bay lobster; specials are featured daily. We also have a great choice of good wines, available by the bottle or the glass, and a selection of locally brewed beers, some produced specially for us.

Stay with us to relax, or to follow one of the seven circular walks through stunning countryside that start from the Inn. Horse riding for experienced riders or complete novices can be arranged. Plenty of parking. Dogs (no charge), children and walkers are very welcome!

Blue Ball Inn formerly The Exmoor Sandpiper Inn
Countisbury, Lynmouth, Devon EX35 6NE
01598 741263
www.BlueBallinn.com • www.exmoorsandpiper.com

SOUTH WEST ENGLAND

Devon 19

Situated in the pretty village of Mortehoe, The Smugglers offers luxury accommodation from twin rooms to family suites.
Treat yourselves and your pets to beautiful coastal walks and golden beaches, before you sample our delicious home-cooked meals, real ales and warm, year round hospitality.

**The Smugglers Rest Inn,
North Morte Road, Mortehoe,
North Devon EX34 7DR
Tel/Fax: 01271 870891**

info@smugglersmortehoe.co.uk
www.smugglersmortehoe.co.uk

8 BEDROOMS, ALL WITH PRIVATE BATHROOM. FREE HOUSE WITH REAL ALE.
CHILDREN AND PETS WELCOME. BAR AND RESTAURANT MEALS. NON-SMOKING AREAS.
ILFRACOMBE 4 MILES. D£.

THE DARTBRIDGE INN
Totnes Road, Buckfastleigh, Devon TQ11 0JR
Tel: 01364 642 214 • www.dartbridgeinn-buckfastleigh.co.uk

With a number of day-trip attractions nearby, this comfortable inn provides ground floor accommodation in a variety of double and twin rooms, with Z-beds and cots available on request. Fine wines and coffees, lunchtime snacks, and dishes featuring locally caught fish are obtainable all day everyday in the bar and restaurant.

Please mention **Pubs & Inns** of Britain
when making enquiries about accommodation featured in these pages

THE BLUE BALL INN (on facing page)

16 BEDROOMS, ALL WITH PRIVATE BATHROOM. ALL BEDROOMS NON-SMOKING. FREE HOUSE WITH REAL ALE.
CHILDREN AND PETS WELCOME. BAR AND RESTAURANT MEALS.
LYNTON 2 MILES. S£££, D££.

PORT LIGHT Hotel, Restaurant & Inn

As featured in *The Times, Guardian, Mail, Telegraph*

- Luxury en suite rooms, easy access onto the gardens
- Close to secluded sandy cove 20 minutes' walk
- No charge for pets which are most welcome throughout the hotel
- Recognised for outstanding food and service with a great reputation for superb home-cooked fayre
- Set alongside the famous National Trust Salcombe to Hope Cove coastal walk
- Fully licensed bar - log burner - real ale
- Large free car park ◆ Open Christmas & New Year
- Self-catering cottages nearby

A totally unique location, set amidst acres of National Trust coastal countryside with panoramic views towards Cornwall, Dartmoor and France.

Bolberry Down, Malborough, Near Salcombe, South Devon TQ7 3DY
e-mail: info@portlight.co.uk • www.portlight.co.uk
Tel: (01548) 561384 or (07970) 859992 • Sean & Hazel Hassall

6 BEDROOMS, ALL WITH PRIVATE BATHROOM. FREE HOUSE WITH REAL ALE. ALL BEDROOMS NON-SMOKING. CHILDREN AND PETS WELCOME. BAR LUNCHES, RESTAURANT EVENINGS ONLY. DESIGNATED COVERED SMOKING AREA. SALCOMBE 2 MILES. D££

Think of moorland, and Devon immediately comes to mind. A county of contrasts, to the north are the wild moors of the Exmoor National Park, fringed by dramatic cliffs and combes, golden beaches and picturesque harbours, with busy market towns and sleepy villages near the coast. For family holidays, one of the best known of the many Blue Flag beaches on the north coast is at Woolacombe, with three miles of sand and a choice of holiday parks. Ilfracombe, originally a Victorian resort, with an annual Victorian festival, provides all kinds of family entertainment. An experience not to be missed is the cliff railway between the pretty little port of Lynmouth and its twin village of Lynton high on the cliff, with a backdrop of dramatic gorges or combes.

In the centre of the county lies Dartmoor, with its wild open spaces, granite tors and spectacular moorland, rich in wildlife and ideal for walking, pony trekking and cycling.

The Channel coast to the south, with its gentle climate and scenery, is an attractive destination at any time of year. The long stretches of beautiful sandy beaches, pebble and shingle are intersected by river estuaries which provide shelter for migrating birds and other wildlife, with fascinating towns full of history.

The Globe Hotel

Topsham, Exeter, Devon EX3 0HR
Tel: 01392 873471

Discover Topsham and Discover The Globe, a Traditional Inn situated in the centre of Topsham, Exeter's Historic and Beautiful Estuary Town.

The Globe has 19 en suite bedrooms, some with four-posters, two ground floor rooms and serviced apartments in a nearby annex.

The Café Restaurant offers a taste of the West Country whilst the Inn Bar serves local ales, wines and juices.

Topsham Ales Community Brewery is housed in The Globe courtyard. Bike hire is available at the Globe's Route 2 Café Bar giving the perfect chance to explore the Exe Estuary. Menus and tariffs are available on the website.

e-mail: sales@globehotel.com • www.globehotel.com

19 BEDROOMS, ALL WITH PRIVATE BATHROOM. ALL BEDROOMS NON-SMOKING. FREE HOUSE WITH REAL ALE. CHILDREN AND PETS WELCOME. BAR AND RESTAURANT MEALS. NON-SMOKING AREAS. EXETER 4 MILES. S££££, D£££.

Please note...

All the information in this book is given in good faith in the belief that it is correct. However, the publishers cannot guarantee the facts given in these pages, neither are they responsible for changes in policy, ownership or terms that may take place after the date of going to press. Readers should always satisfy themselves that the facilities they require are available and that the terms, if quoted, still apply.

Rates

S – SINGLE ROOM rate   D – Sharing DOUBLE/TWIN ROOM

S£ D£ = Under £35   S££ D££ = £36-£45   S£££ D£££ = £46-£55   S££££ D££££ = Over £55

This is meant as an indication only and does not show prices for Special Breaks, Weekends, etc. Guests are therefore advised to verify all prices on enquiring or booking.

Devon — SOUTH WEST ENGLAND

A haven for walkers, riders, fishermen, canoeists or anyone just looking for an opportunity to enjoy the natural beauty of Dartmoor. We specialise in home-made food using local produce wherever possible. With the emphasis on Devon beers and ciders, you have the opportunity to quench your thirst after the efforts of the day with a drink at the bar or relaxing on the chesterfields in the lounge area, complete with log fire for winter evenings. Muddy paws, boots and hooves welcome.

THE FOREST INN

Hexworthy, Dartmoor
PL20 6SD
Tel: 01364 631211
Fax: 01364 631515
e-mail: info@theforestinn.co.uk

10 BEDROOMS, ALL EN SUITE OR WITH PRIVATE BATHROOM. ALL BEDROOMS NON-SMOKING. FREE HOUSE WITH REAL ALE. CHILDREN AND PETS WELCOME. BAR AND RESTAURANT MEALS. ASHBURTON 7 MILES. S£££, D££.

Please note...

All the information in this book is given in good faith in the belief that it is correct. However, the publishers cannot guarantee the facts given in these pages, neither are they responsible for changes in policy, ownership or terms that may take place after the date of going to press. Readers should always satisfy themselves that the facilities they require are available and that the terms, if quoted, still apply.

Looking for holiday accommodation?
for details of hundreds of properties throughout the UK visit:
www.holidayguides.com

SOUTH WEST ENGLAND Dorset 23

Dorset

The Brewers Arms
**Martinstown, Dorchester,
Dorset DT2 9LB
01305 889361
e-mail: jackie_smith54@hotmail.com
www.thebrewersarms.com**

A friendly country pub which provides home cooked food. Popular with ramblers, cyclists and lovers of the English countryside. Walks and bridleways within the village. The coast is roughly a 10 minute drive. Relaxing garden. Skittle alley. Large car park. There is an area where customers can eat and sit with their dogs.

NO ACCOMMODATION.
CHILDREN AND PETS WELCOME. BAR AND RESTAURANT MEALS.
DORCHESTER 3 MILES.

The Castle Inn
Lulworth Cove BH20 5RN

Traditional family-run 16th Century thatched free house pub and hotel. Bed & Breakfast accommodation. Meals from locally sourced products. Local real ales and ciders. Near the beautiful Lulworth Cove & Durdle Door of the Jurassic Coastline and surrounded by the Isle of Purbeck countryside.

Tel: 01929 400311 • www.lulworthinn.com

15 BEDROOMS, 11 WITH PRIVATE BATHROOM. ALL BEDROOMS NON-SMOKING. FREE HOUSE WITH REAL ALE.
CHILDREN AND PETS WELCOME. BAR MEALS.
WOOL 5 MILES. S£££, D££.

Please mention **Pubs & Inns of Britain**
when making enquiries about accommodation featured in these pages

The Fisherman's Haunt

Salisbury Road, Winkton,
Christchurch, Dorset BH23 7AS
Tel: (0)1202 477 283 • Fax: (0)1202 478 883
e-mail: fishermanshaunt@fullers.co.uk • www.fullershotels.com

Originally built as an inn dating back to 1673, this olde worlde property is full of period features, character and charm.

All 12 bedrooms are stylish and furnished to an excellent standard. We take great care in choosing our beds and bed linen, so that our guests have a comfortable and relaxing sleep. The restaurant enjoys an excellent reputation for good home-cooked food, using the finest local produce, good wines and Fuller's award-winning beers.

The Fisherman's Haunt is close to the New Forest, within easy reach of Christchurch and Bournemouth and is ideal for the country lover and angler, with the River Avon being close by.

All our Inns have been assessed and thoroughly inspected by the respected organisation of 'Quality in Tourism'.

Guest review - *A great place to stay. A very comfortable room with a high quality finish to both bedroom and bathroom. Great food for both breakfast and evening meals - good menu with a great selection on the 'specials' board for evening meals. Great location for both coast and New Forest. Would happily stay here again.*

FINDING US BY ROAD
From the M27 follow the signs to Ringwood. Take the B3347 to Sopley and Winkton for about 5 miles – the hotel in on the LH side

SOUTH WEST ENGLAND — Dorset

The Silent Woman Inn
Bere Road, Coldharbour, Wareham, Dorset BH20 7PA
Tel: 01929 552909 • www.thesilentwoman.co.uk

Traditional country inn nestling in the heart of Wareham Forest. Beautiful gardens, log fires in winter. Outdoor covered area for summer evenings. All fresh ingredients, wonderful food. Real ales, good wines. Adults only inside. Children's play area.

NO ACCOMMODATION. HALL & WOODHOUSE HOUSE WITH REAL ALE.
PETS WELCOME. BAR AND RESTAURANT MEALS.
WAREHAM 1 MILE.

St Leonards Hotel
185 Ringwood Road, St Leonards, Dorset BH24 2NP
Tel: 01425 471220 • www.st-leonardshotel-ringwood.co.uk

St Leonards is positioned on the edge of the New Forest, making visits to Ringwood, Bournemouth, and Poole easy and stress-free. The hotel restaurant features a seasonal menu, and guests can enjoy real ales, fine wines, and speciality teas and coffees. Accommodation is in 35 en suite bedrooms, all with modern facilities.

The Antelope Inn
8 High Street, Poole, Dorset BH15 1BP
Tel: 01202 672 029 • www.antelopeinn-poole.co.uk

Just a stone's throw from Poole Quay, from where sightseeing trips to France and the Channel Islands leave frequently. 21 first and second floor bedrooms each have an en suite bathroom, plus modern facilities such as a stereo and widescreen DVD.

Rates

S – SINGLE ROOM rate   D – Sharing DOUBLE/TWIN ROOM

| S£ D£ = Under £35 | S££ D££ = £36-£45 | S£££ D£££ = £46-£55 | S££££ D££££ = Over £55 |

This is meant as an indication only and does not show prices for Special Breaks, Weekends, etc. Guests are therefore advised to verify all prices on enquiring or booking.

THE FISHERMAN'S HAUNT (on facing page)

12 BEDROOMS, ALL WITH PRIVATE BATHROOM.
FULLERS HOUSE WITH REAL ALE. CHILDREN AND PETS WELCOME. BAR AND RESTAURANT MEALS.
BOURNEMOUTH 5 MILES. S££££, D££££.

Gloucestershire

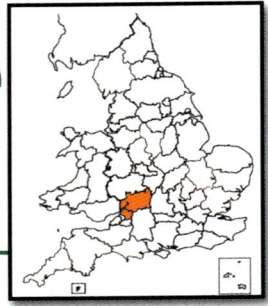

Comfort with a Touch of Character
The Bowl Inn
and Lilies Restaurant
Lower Almondsbury
(next door to St Mary's Church)

12th century Inn offering:

Tastefully furnished en suite accommodation with TV/entertainment system with FREE internet, plus FREE wireless broadband access. Refreshingly different oak-beamed conference room available for your business meeting - also a very popular choice for private parties. Good bar food and real ales served all day.

Mon-Fri: 12noon-2.30pm and 6-10pm • Sat: 12noon-10pm • Sun: 12noon-8pm

Lilies A La Carte Restaurant recently awarded One Rosette by the AA
Open Mon-Fri lunchtime and evenings; Saturday evening and Sunday lunch.

www.thebowlinn.co.uk (including current menus)
5 minutes from Junction 16 M5

16 Church Road, Lower Almondsbury BS32 4DT • 01454 612757

13 BEDROOMS, ALL WITH PRIVATE BATHROOM. ALL BEDROOMS NON-SMOKING. FREE HOUSE WITH REAL ALE. CHILDREN WELCOME. BAR AND RESTAURANT MEALS.
BRISTOL 7 MILES. S£££, D££££.

Old Manse Hotel
Victoria Street, Bourton-on-the-Water, Gloucestershire GL54 2BX
Tel: 01451 820082 • www.oldmansehotel-gloucestershire.co.uk

Ideally set in the centre of the Costwold village of Bourton-on-the-Water is this pretty country hotel, restaurant and pub. Real ales, fine wines and specialty cream teas and coffees are available. For a romantic getaway, book the four-poster room. All bedrooms are en suite, with a unique ambience, and full English breakfast is included in the room rate.

SOUTH WEST ENGLAND
Gloucestershire 27

OLD PASSAGE — *The Seafood Restaurant on the River*
Passage Road, Arlingham GL2 7JR
Tel: 01452 740547

High quality, award-winning seafood restaurant with accommodation. Three double en suite rooms with wonderful views across the River Severn and the Forest of Dean. Outdoor terrace available during summer months.

e-mail: oldpassage@ukonline.co.uk • www.theoldpassage.com

3 BEDROOMS, ALL WITH PRIVATE BATHROOM. ALL BEDROOMS NON-SMOKING. FREE HOUSE WITH REAL ALE. CHILDREN AND PETS WELCOME. RESTAURANT MEALS.
STROUD 9 MILES. S££££, D££££.

THE FOUNTAIN INN & LODGE
Parkend, Royal Forest of Dean, Gloucestershire GL15 4JD

Traditional village inn, well known locally for its excellent meals and real ales.
A Forest Fayre menu offers such delicious main courses as Lamb Shank In Redcurrant and Rosemary Sauce, and Gloucester Sausage in Onion Gravy, together with a large selection of curries, vegetarian dishes, and other daily specials.

Centrally situated in one of England's foremost wooded areas, the inn makes an ideal base for sightseeing, or for exploring some of the many peaceful forest walks nearby.

All bedrooms (including two specially adapted for the less able) are en suite, decorated and furnished to an excellent standard, and have television and tea/coffee making facilities.

Tel: 01594 562189 • Fax: 01594 564438
e-mail: thefountaininn@aol.com • www.thefountaininnandlodge.com

8 BEDROOMS, ALL WITH PRIVATE BATHROOM. ALL BEDROOMS NON-SMOKING. FREE HOUSE WITH REAL ALE. CHILDREN AND PETS WELCOME. BAR AND RESTAURANT MEALS. DESIGNATED COVERED SMOKING AREA.
LYDNEY 4 MILES. S££, D£

Pet-Friendly Pubs, Inns & Hotels
on pages 170-176
These establishments may not feature in the main section of the book

Gloucestershire

The Redesdale Arms was originally a 17th century coaching inn, on the road from Birmingham to London. Now a newly refurbished three star hotel which mixes the traditional concepts of inn keeping with the standards of a modern hotel. Set in delightful market town of Moreton-in-Marsh, you are in the heart of the Cotswolds and within 10-20 minutes of places such as Stow-on-the-Wold, Stratford-upon-Avon, Bourton-on-the-Water and Broadway. Log fires in the winter, patio garden in the summer and a short walk from the rolling Cotswold hills. Open all year. Privately owned and managed. Discounts often available midweek, throughout the year - please ask for details.

THE REDESDALE ARMS
High Street, Moreton-in-Marsh, Gloucestershire GL56 0AW
Tel: 01608 650308 • Fax: 01608 651843
e-mail: info@redesdalearms.com • www.redesdalearms.com

24 BEDROOMS, ALL WITH PRIVATE BATHROOM. ALL BEDROOMS NON-SMOKING. FREE HOUSE WITH REAL ALE. CHILDREN WELCOME. BAR AND RESTAURANT MEALS.
CHIPPING NORTON 8 MILES. S££££, D££££.

The Roo Bar
Clifton Down Station, Whiteladies Road, Bristol, Gloucestershire BS8 2PN
Tel: 0117 9237204

Just a short distance from the city centre, this Aussie theme pub is predominantly a sports bar with a number of screens showing live sporting fixtures. Other facilities include two American pool tables, a well stocked bar and an imaginative menu of pub favourites.

The Bay Horse
1 Lewins Mead, Bristol, Gloucestershire BS1 2LJ • Tel: 01179 258287

Conveniently situated in Bristol's city centre, this drinking and dining venue offers tasty meals, plus fine wines and real ales. There is karaoke every Friday and facilities include a non-smoking area and a large screen TV.

THE CLOSE HOTEL
Long Street, Tetbury, Gloucestershire GL8 8AQ
Tel: 01666 502 272 • www.theclose-hotel.com

This remarkable hotel stands second-to-none in terms of 16th century elegance, and enjoys a flawless reputation for atmosphere and comfort. There is a stylish restaurant offering a superb dining experience, and a well maintained garden with central fountain. All rooms are en suite; for an extra touch of luxury two have antique four-poster beds.

Somerset

This small 14th century hotel, set in the only street in Dunster and within the Exmoor National Park, is an escapist's paradise. The 28 en suite bedrooms have Freeview TV, tea/coffee making facilities and hairdryers, some have four-posters and we have a selection of superior rooms.

In the intimate Luttrell Arms Restaurant, menus feature the best of modern British cuisine, while the bar, a traditional pub with log fires provides the same choice in a less formal atmosphere.

**The Luttrell Arms,
High Street, Dunster
TA24 6SG
Tel: 01643 821555
Fax: 01643 821567
info@luttrellarms.fsnet.co.uk
www.luttrellarms.co.uk**

28 BEDROOMS, ALL WITH PRIVATE BATHROOM. FREE HOUSE WITH REAL ALE. ALL BEDROOMS NON-SMOKING. CHILDREN AND PETS WELCOME. BAR AND RESTAURANT MEALS. NON-SMOKING AREAS. MINEHEAD 2 MILES. S££££, D£££.

THE HOOD ARMS (on next page)

12 BEDROOMS, ALL WITH PRIVATE BATHROOM. ALL BEDROOMS NON-SMOKING. FREE HOUSE WITH REAL ALE. CHILDREN AND PETS WELCOME. BAR AND RESTAURANT MEALS. DESIGNATED COVERED SMOKING AREA. NETHER STOWEY 3 MILES. S££££, D££££.

THE Hood Arms

A famous 17th century coaching Inn. Situated on the A39 at the foot of the Quantock Hills, close to the spectacular fossil beach at Kilve, a paradise for walkers, mountain bikers, dogs, sporting parties or simply relaxing.

The 12 recently refurbished en suite bedrooms include stylish four-posters. Stag Lodge in the courtyard garden has two luxury bedrooms and sitting room.

The beamed restaurant offers a relaxed dining experience whilst providing delicious locally sourced food. A full à la carte menu, chef's specials and bar snacks are available 7 days a week.

The bar is full of character and boasts an impressive array of real ales.

A warm welcome awaits locals and traveller alike. Dogs welcome.

Please look at our website for more details and prices.

Kilve Beach

The Hood Arms, Kilve, Bridgwater, Somerset TA5 1EA
01278 741210 • Fax: 01278 741477
e-mail: info@thehoodarms.com
www.thehoodarms.com

The Talbot
15th Century Coaching Inn
at Mells, Near Frome BA11 3PN

Set in the enchanting Somerset village of Mells, the historic Talbot Inn offers beautiful en suite accommodation, an award-winning restaurant and all the charm of a traditional English inn.

Close to some of the country's most popular attractions, including Bath, Longleat, Cheddar and Wells, the Talbot Inn is the perfect base for exploring this charming corner of England.

Traditional comforts and modern convenience combine to make the Talbot Inn the ideal place for a relaxing weekend break or a base for exploring the beautiful countryside and historic towns and villages around Somerset and Bath. An ideal area for walkers, cyclists and golfers.

All our rooms are named after characters from the history of Mells - from Little Jack Horner to the poet Siegfried Sassoon, and offer supreme comfort and thoughtful amenities.

Dining here offers an award-winning à la carte menu of traditional English food with a delicate French influence, sourced from the best local ingredients. The informal restaurant offers a backdrop of extremes, with low oak beams and ceiling hops the alternative to a front room that would grace any country house hotel.

On sunny days, enjoy al fresco dining in the garden area. Our overnight guests are served a freshly cooked English breakfast, whilst the Talbot's Sunday lunch has become a Mells institution.

Tel: 01373 812254
enquiries@talbotinn.com
www.talbotinn.com

THE HALFWAY HOUSE INN COUNTRY LODGE

Chilthorne Domer,
Near Yeovil,
Somerset
BA22 8RE
Tel: 01935 840350
Fax: 01935 849006
paul@halfwayhouseinn.com
www.halfwayhouseinn.net

Offering you the very best in country hospitality and an ideal base from which to tour Somerset and Dorset, The Halfway House Inn Country Lodge has 20 en suite rooms available, including a disabled-friendly lodge and a charming four-poster Bridal Suite with jacuzzi and luxury steam/shower cabinet. All rooms have Sky TV, tea/coffee facilities.
Free wireless internet is available.
Also available is a Function Room with a sit down capacity of 100 people, suitable for engagements, weddings, christenings, family parties or conferences. Barbecue patio with stunning outlook.
Good pub food is available in the restaurant, with a menu to suit all tastes and a frequently changing specials board.
Set within the grounds of The Halfway and with delightful views of the surrounding countryside, there is a fishing and model boating lake. Guests who stay at The Halfway are welcome to sail or fish for free.

The Boathouse
Newbridge Road, Bath, Somerset BA1 3NB • Tel: 01225 482584

The Boathouse is situated by the water's edge and features a well maintained garden, perfect for outdoors enthusiasts in summer months. The interior layout is contemporary and open-plan in style, and the bar stocks a good choice of wines, beers, and real ales. The main menu offers a variety of home cooked meals and pub snacks are available.

The George Inn
Mill Lane, Bathampton, Bath, Somerset BA2 6QB • Tel: 01225 425079

Situated near the River Avon and the Tennyson Avon Canal, the George affords delightful views of the river and boats. The interior is traditional in style, with oak beams, open fires and little alcoves, nooks and crannies. The menu offers a good range of specials including fish dishes, and the Sunday roast lunch is deservedly popular.

The Bristol Inn
Chapel Hill, Clevedon, Somerset BS21 7NL • Tel: 01275 872073

There's never a dull day here at the Bristol Inn, located in the heart of Clevedon village and just a short walk from the beach. A wide choice of beers and ales is available behind the bar, and there is regular entertainment, with live music/disco on Fridays. Facilities include a pool table, dart board, terraced seating and a snug area.

The Who'd A Thought It Inn
Northload Street, Glastonbury, Somerset BA6 9JJ
Tel: 01458 834460 • Fax: 01458 834460 • www.whodathoughtit.co.uk

Interestingly named inn located in the pretty market town of Glastonbury. The smart bar is stocked with a variety of chilled draught beers and the elegant restaurant serves classic English cuisine - diners are advised to book in advance to avoid disappointment.

HALFWAY HOUSE INN COUNTRY LODGE (on facing page)

20 BEDROOMS, ALL EN SUITE. ALL BEDROOMS NON-SMOKING. FREE HOUSE WITH REAL ALE. WELL BEHAVED CHILDREN AND PETS WELCOME. BAR AND RESTAURANT MEALS. DESIGNATED OUTDOOR COVERED SMOKING AREA. YEOVIL 3 MILES. S£££, D££.

THE TALBOT INN (on previous page)

8 BEDROOMS, ALL WITH PRIVATE BATHROOM. FREE HOUSE WITH REAL ALE. CHILDREN AND PETS WELCOME. BAR AND RESTAURANT MEALS. BATH 10 MILES.

Wiltshire

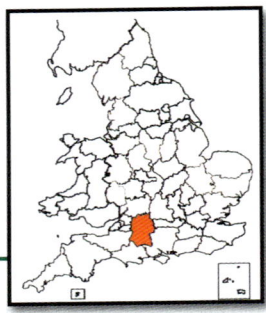

This charming 17th century Cotswold-stone country inn offers comfortable accommodation and delicious home-cooked food. There are two twin bedrooms, a family room and three double rooms, one of which has a traditional four-poster bed; all are en suite (bath or shower) with colour television, tea and coffee making facilities, and radio alarm. In the bar, a fine range of wines, spirits and traditional ales is available, which you can enjoy in front of open log fires. The historic town of Bath is nearby, and many places of interest are within easy reach, such as Stonehenge, Avebury, Stow-on-the-Wold and other famous Cotswold towns.

THE NEELD ARMS INN
The Street, Grittleton,
Wiltshire SN14 6AP
Tel: 01249 782470 • Fax: 01249 782358
info@neeldarms.co.uk
www.neeldarms.co.uk

6 BEDROOMS, ALL WITH PRIVATE BATHROOM. FREE HOUSE WITH REAL ALE. CHILDREN AND PETS WELCOME. BAR AND RESTAURANT MEALS (EVENINGS). NON-SMOKING AREAS. CHIPPENHAM 6 MILES. S£££, D££££.

Rates

S – SINGLE ROOM rate   D – Sharing DOUBLE/TWIN ROOM

S£ D£ = Under £35   S££ D££ = £36-£45   S£££ D£££ = £46-£55   S££££ D££££ = Over £55

This is meant as an indication only and does not show prices for Special Breaks, Weekends, etc. Guests are therefore advised to verify all prices on enquiring or booking.

SOUTH WEST ENGLAND
Wiltshire

The Lamb Inn
High Street, Hindon, Wiltshire SP3 6DP
Tel: 01747 820573 • Fax: 01747 820605
www.lambathindon.co.uk

The fascinating history of this ancient inn is related in its brochure, which reveals among other intriguing facts that it was once the headquarters of a notorious smuggler. No such unlawful goings-on today – just good old-fashioned hospitality in the finest traditions of English inn-keeping. Charmingly furnished single, double and four-poster bedrooms provide overnight guests with cosy country-style accommodation, and the needs of the inner man (or woman!) will be amply satisfied by the varied, good quality meals served in the bar and restaurant. Real ales can be enjoyed in the friendly bar, where crackling log fires bestow charm and atmosphere as well as warmth.

ETC/AA ★★★★

17 BEDROOMS, ALL WITH PRIVATE BATHROOM. ALL BEDROOMS NON-SMOKING. YOUNGS HOUSE WITH REAL ALE. CHILDREN AND PETS WELCOME. BAR AND RESTAURANT MEALS. DESIGNATED COVERED SMOKING AREA SHAFTESBURY 7 MILES. S£££ELL, D£££ELL.

The Rowden Arms
Rowden Hill, Chippenham, Wiltshire SN15 2AW
Tel: 01249 653870

A welcoming family food house, voted number one by the local newspaper. The bar stocks a good range of draught beers, ales and wines and there is a regular programme of entertainment.

The Green Dragon
26 High Street, Market Lavington, Devizes, Wiltshire SN10 4AG
Tel: 01380 813235 • www.greendragonlavington.co.uk

An award-winning inn, with a good selection of real ales, lagers, beers and fine wines, and a superior reputation for food and accommodation. Facilities include an enclosed garden with a pets section and a BBQ area.

THE SMOKING DOG
62 High Street, Malmesbury, Wiltshire SN16 9AT
Tel: 01666 825823

A cosy pub built from Cotswold stone, where the popular menu is prepared from fresh ingredients, and a wide range of fine wines and real ales is available.

The Carpenter's Arms
Easton Town, Sherston, Malmesbury, Wiltshire SN16 0LS
Tel: 01666 840665

'Simple is as simple does' – and never has such a motto been as true as in this pub, which has no jukebox, satellite TV or one-arm bandits. Food is served throughout the day, and facilities include a beer garden and a cosy conservatory.

London
(Central & Greater)

Big Ben and the Houses of Parliament from the London Eye

The Royal Oak
Longbridge Road, Barking, Greater London IG11 8UF
Tel: 020 8507 1600 • www.pub-explorer.com/gtlondon/pub/royaloakbarking.htm

An friendly establishment offering a wide range of draught beers and real ales, plus DJs every Friday and Saturday and regular 70s/80s nights. There are BBQs in summer and live sporting fixtures shown on plasma screens. Over 18s only.

The Coach & Horses
Burnhill Road, Beckenham, Greater London BR3 3LA • **Tel: 0208 6509142**
www.pub-explorer.com/gtlondon/pub/coach&horsesbeckenham.htm

A small likeable pub situated near the beautiful gardens in Kelsey Park. It offers a great selection of draught beers including Guinness and Strongbow, as well as regular and guest real ales. Patio area; wheelchair access throughout.

The Blue Anchor
Bridgen Road, Bexley, Greater London DA5 1JE
Tel: 01322 523582 • www.pub-explorer.com/gtlondon/pub/blueanchorbexley.htm

Good honest beer, real ales and hearty meals are served in this lively pub restaurant. Facilities include an IT box, jukebox, dartboard and pool tables. plus live sporting fixtures shown on plasma screens for that all-important match. A children's menu is available.

The George
74 Bexley High Street, Bexley, Greater London DA5 1AJ
Tel: 01322 523843 • www.pub-explorer.com/gtlondon/pub/georgebexley.htm

A sports bar with a wide selection of cold draught beers and real ales. There's no chance of missing out on an important match, with live sporting fixtures shown on the numerous TVs positioned throughout. Enjoy the quality burger menu and live monthly entertainment. Outdoor eating area available.

The King's Arms
156 The Broadway, Bexleyheath, Greater London DA6 7DW • Tel: 020 8303 1173

All on one level, this busy pub serves breakfast, steaks and a variety of other meals throughout the day. The bar stocks a wide selection of draught beers and fine wines. Regular events include a Monday dart team, Tuesday quiz night and Wednesday poker league. Wifi throughout and a jukebox.

The Yacht
Long Lane, Bexleyheath, Greater London DA7 5AE
Tel: 020 8303 4889 • www.pub-explorer.com/gtlondon/pub/yachtbexleyheath.htm

Customers can expect faultless service at this Steak and Ale house, famed for its airy, open plan arrangement as well as the mouth-watering dishes on offer. Children can amuse themselves in the designated play area while you relax over a fine wine or real ale. Activities include pool night on Tuesday, quiz night on Thursday and two pool tables.

The Crown
155 Bromley Common, Bromley, Greater London BR2 9RJ
Tel: 020 8460 1472 • www.pub-explorer.com/gtlondon/pub/crownbromley.htm

Situated just 2.5 miles from Bromley town centre, the pub restaurant's contemporary interior attracts a large variety of customers in search of a chilled pint, ale, coffee, or food from the full à la carte menu; children's menu also available. Facilities include a quiet area, patio area, baby changing facilities and disabled toilet.

Freelands Tavern
31 Freelands Road, Bromley, Greater London BR1 3HZ • Tel: 020 8464 2296
www.pub-explorer.com/gtlondon/pub/freelandstavernbromley.htm

The Freelands is known for its firm commitment to sport, screening all major fixtures on impressive plasma screens. A great selection of hot and cold food is also available – toasties, jacket potatoes, rib-eye steaks etc. The bar serves a good selection of draught beers, wines and real ales. A popular beer garden is perfect during the summer months.

Shortlands Tavern
Station Road, Shortlands, Bromley, Greater London BR2 0EY
Tel: 020 8460 2770 • www.pub-explorer.com/gtlondon/pub/shortlandstavern.htm

Shortlands is situated next to the railway station and overlooks the platform. Relax in the beer garden over one of the carefully selected wines, beers and ales, or get involved in one of the pub's weekly activities – quiz night, speed pool, or dart. Sports fans can watch that all-important match on the big screen. Children are welcome (till 7pm).

The Rose & Crown
55 High Street, Wimbledon Village, London SW19 5BA
Tel: 020 8947 4713 • Fax: 020 8947 4994 • www.roseandcrownwimbledon.co.uk

Situated within walking distance of the All England Lawn Tennis Club, Wimbledon Theatre and Wimbledon Common, with good train links to central London. Enjoy a cold draught beer or real ale at the friendly bar, dine in comfort inside the snug restaurant or in the airy, heated courtyard. 13 en suite rooms, all with plasma Sky TV, and coffee/tea making facilities.

The Windmill on The Common
Clapham, London SW4 9DE
Tel: 020 8673 4578 • www.windmillclapham.co.uk

A friendly public house blended with a modern hotel, the newly furbished Windmill serves a good range of beers and lagers on tap and boasts a new à la carte menu, with specials changed daily. Accommodation is in 29 luxurious en suite air-conditioned rooms, equipped with king-size beds, plasma screens, freeview TV, fresh milk and wifi.

White Cross Hotel Pub
Riverside (Off Waterlane), Richmond, Surrey TW9 1TH
Tel: 020 8940 6844 • www.youngs.co.uk

Patrons are eagerly encouraged to sample the wide range of Young's award-winning real ales, wines and food. This is the ideal place to go for a cool pint and light bite after the rugby. Facilities include wifi, a beer garden, and log fire

Looking for holiday accommodation?
for details of hundreds of properties throughout the UK visit:

www.holidayguides.com

LONDON & SOUTH EAST ENGLAND

Wheatsheaf Pub
6 Stoney Street, Borough, London SE1 9AA • Tel: 020 7407 7242

Young's have refurbished this tiny market pub and stocked it with a good range of beer. Its two-bar concept has been retained - public and saloon. Enjoy a tipple by the crackling log fire on a winter evening. It is within walking distance of Clink Prison Museum and Southwark Cathedral, as well as the new art-house clubs by London Bridge station.

Westminster Arms
Storey's Gate, Westminster, London SW1P 3AT • Tel: 020 7222 8520

Take a trip to the heart of Westminster for one of many real ales stocked at this pub-restaurant-wine bar. This three-floored establishment, located near to Big Ben, is popular with local office workers. Snacks are available at the bar but for a more relaxing meal, dine upstairs or outside at street level and people watch. The pub is reputedly haunted by the ghost of a boy who died in the Great Fire of London!

The Warrington Hotel
93 Warrington Crescent, Maida Vale, London W9 1EH
Tel: 020 7286 2929 • www.gordonramsay.com/thewarrington

When this pub became an object of chef Gordon Ramsay's affections, there was no turning back ... and who would want to? Guests are of course guaranteed a feast from the exquisite menu. For lovers of fine wine and beer (and a casual dress code) – make the Warrington your next destination.

London has everything to offer! With a range of accommodation at prices to suit every pocket, it's easy to spend a weekend here or take a longer break. Among the most popular places for visitors are the museums and art galleries. The National Gallery houses one of the largest collections in the world, while the Tate Modern concentrates on the work of artists from the beginning of the 20th century. Except for some special exhibitions, entry to both is free, and this also applies to the Natural History Museum, where a new Darwin Centre has opened and the Victoria and Albert Museum, with such a wide range of exhibits of art and design from different cultures. Smaller, more specialised museums exist too, including the Old Operating Theatre and Herb Garret, a real operating theatre dating from 1821, and the Movieum of London, the film museum where you have the opportunity to shoot your own film, and to see props used in Superman and other favourite films.

Viaduct Tavern
126 Newgate St, Holborn, London EC1A 7AA
Tel: 020 7600 1863

Located opposite the Holborn Viaduct, this little corner pub offers customers a relaxed environment away from the hustle and bustle in which to enjoy real ales, wines and beers. Sandwiches are available Monday to Friday at lunchtimes. Original features date back to 1869, the year Queen Victoria opened the Holborn Viaduct. Nearest Tube – St Paul's.

Trafalgar Tavern
Park Row, Greenwich, London SE10 9NW • Tel: 020 8858 2909
www.trafalgartavern.co.uk

Charles Dickens and William Gladstone once frequented this Regency-style drinking house. After a major refurbishment the Trafalgar is now much more than just a pub, with a restaurant and bar. Snacks are available and mouth-watering fish dishes are a 'must try'.

Town of Ramsgate
62 Wapping High Street, London E1W 2PN • Tel: 020 7481 8000

This narrow pub has a murky but interesting past. Situated next to the Wapping Old Stairs, an alleyway that leads down to the riverside, one can quite believe that convicts would use the narrow path as an escape route all those years ago. Now it is a welcoming local for East Londoners and visiting friends.

THE TOTTENHAM
6 Oxford Street, London W1D 1AN • Tel: 020 7636 7201

Believe it or not, the Tottenham is the last remaining pub out of the 38 that used to exist on London's famous Oxford Street, and was built by the famous Baker Brothers. This is the ideal place to go after work for a quick pint to unwind from the day's stresses.

Tom Cribb
36 Panton Street, London SW1Y 4EA • Tel: 020 7839 3801 • www.pubs.com

Come to Tom Cribb's and spot performers from the local 'luvvie' hinterland. Named after Tom Cribb himself, the bare-knuckle fighter turned publican, this traditional Piccadilly pub serves a good range of beers and ales on tap. Come in for a hearty meal, light sandwich or jacket potato. Facilities include TV and air-conditioning.

The Tipperary
66 Fleet St, London EC4Y 1HT
Tel: 020 75836470

Situated on London's Fleet Street, this authentic Irish pub serves Guinness with a smile. The pub is open all day, with wheelchair access and real ales!

The Ship
116 Wardour Street, Soho, London W1F 0TT
Tel: 020 7437 8446

Come and immerse yourself in the creative atmosphere of this Soho pub - Wardour Street is the centre of the TV and film-making industry and The Ship is popular with many in the business. The bar is well stocked with Fuller's draught and real ales.

RED LION PUB
48 Parliament Street, Whitehall, London SW1A 2NH
Tel: 020 7930 5826

Situated between the House of Commons and Downing Street, The Red Lion is popular with politicians, civil servants and journalists. An upstairs dining room and cellar bar provide extra space for busy times of day.

Richard I Pub
52 Royal Hill, Greenwich, London SE10 8RT
Tel: 020 8692 2996

Located on a quiet back street in Greenwich is this charming 1920s conversion, offering two bar areas, and a beer garden for BBQs, al fresco drinking and dining in summer months. The menu ranges from ciabattas and sandwiches to big burgers, jacket potatoes, fish and chips and chilli con carne. Children are welcome till 8.30pm.

Red Lion
Crown Passage, Off Pall Mall, St James's, London SW1Y 6PP
Tel: 020 7930 4141

This pub can get very busy but it is deservedly popular. The bar stocks a good selection of whiskies and beers, and for a light bite, filling sandwiches at affordable prices. The surrounding are area retains a genial Dickensian ambience, particularly as it is still gas lit!

Punch Bowl Pub
41 Farm St, Mayfair, London W1J 5RP
Tel: 020 7493 6841

The Punch Bowl is a enjoyably understated little pub situated in London's Mayfair. Simple decorations outside and inside mean there's no risk of pretentiousness or over-priced drinks and food - ideal for time out whether working or sightseeing.

Prince Alfred Pub
5a Formosa Street, Maida Vale, London W9 1EE • Tel: 020 7286 3287
www.theprincealfred.com

This is one of the last remaining authentic Victorian pubs, Grade II Listed. So class conscious were the Victorians that pubs such as this were built compartmentally, each of the five bars having a separate entrance. At the back, there is a dining room with a bar.

Berkshire

The Greyhound
Eton Wick, Berkshire SL4 6JE
Tel: 01753 863925

A picturesque pub with plenty of walks close by • Real ale • Food served daily • Sunday lunch served between 12 noon – 3pm.

NO ACCOMMODATION   REAL ALE.
BAR MEALS.
ETON 1 MILE, SLOUGH 2 MILES.

THE WEE WAIF
Old Bath Road, Charvil, Near Reading, Berkshire RG10 9RJ
Tel: 0118 9440 066 • www.weewaif-hotel.co.uk

Situated in the tranquil village of Charvil, with easy access to Reading, London and Heathrow. The restaurant is open seven days a week and features a daily-changing specials board. A range of accommodation will suit all requirements, with Sky TV, en suite bath and shower, and extra linen. Newbury racecourse is just 40 minutes away.

Rates
S – SINGLE ROOM rate   D – Sharing DOUBLE/TWIN ROOM

S£ D£ = Under £35   S££ D££ = £36-£45   S£££ D£££ = £46-£55   S££££ D££££ = Over £55

This is meant as an indication only and does not show prices for Special Breaks, Weekends, etc. Guests are therefore advised to verify all prices on enquiring or booking.

The Dundas Arms

53 Station Road, Kintbury RG17 9UT
Tel: 01488 658263 • Fax: 01488 658568

Set in an Area of Outstanding Natural Beauty on the banks of the Kennet and Avon Canal this welcoming inn has provided sustenance for the hungry and thirsty traveller since the end of the 18th century. Five en suite bedrooms situated on the ground floor, all with patio doors leading to the terrace overlooking the River Kennet. Restaurant and bar meals available.

Bed and Full English Breakfast from £80 single, £90 double.

e-mail: info@dundasarms.co.uk • www.dundasarms.co.uk

5 BEDROOMS, ALL WITH PRIVATE BATHROOM. FREE HOUSE WITH REAL ALE. ALL BEDROOMS NON-SMOKING. CHILDREN WELCOME. BAR AND RESTAURANT MEALS.
HUNGERFORD 3 MILES. S££££, D££

The Wellington Arms

203 Yorktown Road, Sandhurst, Berkshire GU47 9BN
Tel: 01252 872408
www.thewellingtonarms.co.uk

The Wellington Arms is a friendly, inviting local pub with en suite B&B accommodation, situated in the heart of Sandhurst.

Public bar, spacious lounge bar and spacious gardens; large car park.

Here at the Wellington Arms we provide a large selection of foods to cater for most tastes and appetites. We source the majority of our meats and vegetables from the local area, ensuring optimum quality whilst also helping reduce our carbon footprint.

Welcome to The Wellington Arms and enjoy your visit!

6 BEDROOMS, ALL WITH PRIVATE BATHROOM. ALL BEDROOMS NON-SMOKING. BRAKSPEAR HOUSE WITH REAL ALE. CHILDREN WELCOME, PETS IN FRONT BAR ONLY. BAR MEALS. DESIGNATED COVERED SMOKING AREA.
CAMBERLEY 3 MILES. S££££, D££.

THE BUNK INN (on next page)

7 BEDROOMS, ALL WITH PRIVATE BATHROOM. CHILDREN WELCOME, PETS IN BAR ONLY. BAR AND RESTAURANT MEALS. NON-SMOKING AREAS.
NEWBURY 3 MILES. S££££, D££££.

Buckinghamshire

DIFFERENT DRUMMER HOTEL
High Street, Stony Stratford, Milton Keynes, Bucks MK11 1AH
Tel: 01908 564733 • Fax: 01908 260646
info@hoteldifferentdrummer.co.uk
www.hoteldifferentdrummer.co.uk

Until 1982 known as 'The Swan with Two Necks', this ancient inn has been transformed into a superbly furnished hotel, where the comfortable guest rooms have en suite bathrooms, colour television with satellite channels, free wireless internet access, tea/coffee making etc. In the magnificent, oak-panelled Al Tamborista Restaurant diners may experience by candlelight Italian and seafood cuisine at its very best and most inventive. Also very deserving of mention is the recently opened wine bar and restaurant, The Vine, where top international cuisine and quality wines combine with London-style contemporary chic. An absolute must for those looking for something different in style and cuisine.

19 BEDROOMS, ALL EN SUITE. ALL BEDROOMS NON-SMOKING. CHILDREN WELCOME.
BAR AND RESTAURANT MEALS.
LONDON 45 MILES. S£££/££££, D££££.

Ye Old Jug
Lower Rd, Hardwick, Aylesbury, Buckinghamshire HP22 4DZ
Tel: 01296 641303

With easy links to nearby London and Oxford, this delightful establishment offers a wide variety of activities throughout the year. Facilities include a beer garden, indoor and outdoor function areas, a large plasma TV and wifi access throughout.

The Saracen's Head Inn
38 Whielden Street, Amersham Old Town, Bucks HP7 0HU
Tel: 01494 721958 • www.thesaracensheadinn.com

Hear the chilling tale of the two ghosts who reputedly roam this 17th century inn at night. With an outdoor area for BBQs and an open log fire in the bar area, this charming English pub provides a unique ambience. Lunch and evening meals are available in the restaurant and accommodation includes single, double and family size rooms.

Gatehanger's Freehouse
Lower End, Ashendon, Aylesbury, Bucks HP18 0HE
Tel: 01296 651296 • www.gatehangers.co.uk

This traditional countryside inn is situated just a short drive from Aylesbury village, with neighbouring Oxford close by. The five en suite bedrooms offer coffee and tea making facilities, and the restaurant serves home-cooked food made from local produce, with bar snacks available Friday lunchtimes and a weekly Sunday roast.

BROUGHTON HOTEL
Broughton, Milton Keynes, Buckinghamshire MK10 9AA
Tel: 01908 667726 • www.broughtonhotel-miltonkeynes.co.uk

Ideal for a stopover and fully equipped with amenities to keep the whole family entertained, with five plasma screens, a beer garden/patio area and children's play area. The restaurant provides an extensive menu, with a Wednesday curry night. All rooms have recently been decorated and have an en suite shower and bath.

Only half an hour from London, the rolling hills and wooded valleys of the Buckinghamshire countryside provide a wonderful contrast to city life. Enjoy the bluebells in spring and the autumn colours of the woodland while following the innumerable footpaths, bridleways and National Trails that cross the county, looking at the local flora and fauna on the way.

There are fascinating historic towns and villages, including West Wycombe, owned by the National Trust, which also has many other interesting properties in the area. These include the stunning gardens at Cliveden, former home of the Astors and focus of the early twentieth century social scene. Shoppers will want to visit the complex at High Wycombe or for more specialised outlets, Amersham, the Georgian market town of Marlow, or Stony Stratford. Outdoors or in, there's plenty of choice in Buckinghamshire.

LONDON & SOUTH EAST ENGLAND — Buckinghamshire

www.churchhousehotel.co.uk
Church House Hotel
**50 Rowsham Dell, Giffard Park
Milton Keynes
Buckinghamshire
MK14 5SJ**

- *All rooms en suite, with Sky TV, tea/coffee making, radio alarm, hairdryer and direct-dial telephone.*
- **Homely atmosphere**
- **TV Lounge • Games room**
- **Restaurant/Bar**
- **Functions and parties**
- **Conferences**
- **Ample car parking**

Tel: 01908 216030 • Fax: 01908 216332 • info@churchhousehotel.co.uk

10 BEDROOMS, ALL WITH PRIVATE BATHROOM. ALL BEDROOMS NON-SMOKING. FREE HOUSE. CHILDREN AND PETS WELCOME. BAR AND RESTAURANT MEALS. LONDON 45 MILES. S£££, D££££.

The Five Arrows
**Waddesdon, Near Aylesbury, Buckinghamshire HP18 0JE
Tel: 01296 651727 • Fax: 01296 655716
e-mail: five.arrows@nationaltrust.org.uk • www.thefivearrows.co.uk**

This charming small country hotel and restaurant stands at the gates of Waddesdon Manor. It was originally built by Baron Ferdinand de Rothschild to house the craftsmen and architects working on the Manor. There are nine en suite bedrooms and two suites. The bar and restaurant are open seven days a week. Lunch or dinner is a relaxed, informal experience, and on fine days may be enjoyed in the pretty courtyard and garden. It has a reputation for imaginative modern European food, with a wine list featuring a wide range of Rothschild wines.

*Open for breakfast, morning coffee, lunch, afternoon tea and dinner
Sunday lunches are served from 12 noon to 3.30pm • Children welcome*

11 BEDROOMS, ALL WITH PRIVATE BATHROOM. ALL BEDROOMS NON-SMOKING. FREE HOUSE WITH REAL ALE. CHILDREN WELCOME. RESTAURANT MEALS. AYLESBURY 5 MILES. S££££, D££££.

FREE or **REDUCED RATE** entry to Holiday Visits and Attractions – see our **READERS' OFFER VOUCHERS** on pages 179-204

Hampshire

The Swan Hotel
High Street, Alton, Hampshire GU34 1AT
Tel: 01420 83777 • Fax: 01420 87975 • www.swanhotel-alton.co.uk

Jane Austen afficionados can enjoy a visit to her cottage in nearby Chawton, now a museum displaying her life's work. With a lavishly decorated interior and well furnished bedrooms, The Swan is an ideal place to stay. Thes 36 en suite rooms have colour TV, tea/coffee making facilities, and wifi throughout.

The Hen & Chicken
Upper Froyle, Alton, Hampshire GU34 4JH
Tel: 01420 22115 • www.henandchicken.co.uk

On the A31, a friendly establishment where children are welcome, with their own special play area. Traditional features include an inglenook fireplace and a large beer garden, and the food menu includes classic dishes and pub meals. The well stocked bar offers wines, beers and real ales.

The Danebury Hotel
2 High Street, Andover, Hampshire SP10 1NX
Tel: 01264 323 332 • 01264 335 440 • www.daneburyhotel-andover.co.uk

Just a short drive from Stonehenge is this luxurious town house hotel which dates back centuries. These days it is the place to go at weekends, with a busy disco and late bar. Relax after lunch or dinner with a glass of wine on one of the soft leather sofas in the The Market Bar. Guests can expect high quality accommodation with amenities including satellite TV.

Pet-Friendly Pubs, Inns & Hotels
on pages 170-176
These establishments may not feature in the main section of the book

THE WHITE BUCK (on facing page)

7 BEDROOMS, ALL WITH PRIVATE BATHROOM. FULLERS HOUSE WITH REAL ALE. CHILDREN AND PETS WELCOME. BAR AND RESTAURANT MEALS.
RINGWOOD 4 MILES. S££££, D££££.

The White Buck

Bisterne Close,
Burley, Ringwood,
Hampshire BH24 4AT
Tel:(0) 1425 402 264 • Fax:(0)1425 403 588
e-mail: whitebuck@fullers.co.uk • www.fullershotels.com

A former country house with seven stylish refurbished bedrooms, The White Buck is set in two and a half acres in the heart of the New Forest, a wonderful location for a relaxing stay. Well known for fine food and Fuller's cask ales, the inn combines rustic charm with a traditional atmosphere and attractive period-style bars. Wedding receptions, dinner parties and small social events catered for. Please call the inn for further information or menus.

All our Inns have been assessed and thoroughly inspected by the respected organisation of 'Quality in Tourism'.

Guest review – *"I cannot commend the staff of the White Buck inn enough. Everyone we had contact with from reception to bar staff seemed to have one aim in common which was to ensure that their guests were well looked after. Superb place."*

FINDING US BY ROAD... Situated between A31 & A35. Follow signs for Burley Village. The White Buck is signposted just on the outskirts of the village.

The Three Lions

Stuckton, near Fordingbridge, Hampshire SP6 2HF

Tel: 01425 652489 • Fax: 01425 656144

Welcome to The Three Lions, a gem in the New Forest National Park.

Within this beautiful setting, a place in which to relax with good food and fine wines, to come and go as you please, without the formality of a hotel.

All bedrooms are en suite, overlooking the gardens and beyond to the forest. Hot tub and Sauna. Ground floor accommodation with ease of access for less mobile guests.

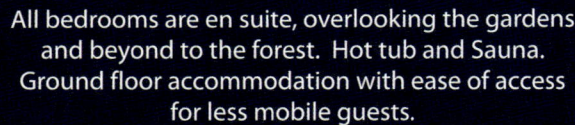

Local attractions include the New Forest, the Dorset and Hampshire coastline with coastal walks and sandy beaches, and the cathedral cities of Salisbury and Winchester.

Family activities nearby include a leisure pool centre, Marwell Zoo, Paulton's Fun Park and Beaulieu Car Museum.

Award winning restaurant, accommodation and excellent facilities, ideal for enjoying a stress relieving short break or for a discreet business meeting.

Three times Hampshire 'Restaurant of the Year', (Good Food Guide).

National Newcomer of the Year (Good Hotel Guide)

Michelin rated

www.thethreelionsrestaurant.co.uk

The Bear Hotel
15-17 East Street, Havant, Hampshire PO9 1AA
Tel: 02392 486 501 • Fax: 02392 470 551 • www.bearhotel-havant.co.uk

The Bear is positioned close to the town centre, and boasts a host of famous past guests, including Queen Victoria, Churchill and Eisenhower. Accommodation and food are matched in terms of quality and comfort; the restaurant is renowned in the area for serving excellent traditional fare. Single, double, twin and family rooms are available, all en suite.

The Raven Hotel
Station Road, Hook, Hampshire RG27 9HS
Tel: 01256 762 541 • Fax: 01256 768 677 • www.ravenhotel-hook.co.uk

Former guests of this elegant hotel include Enid Blyton and Edward VIII. It enjoys a convenient position half an hour away from Windsor Castle, the New Forest, Bird World, Ascot, Windsor and Newbury racecourses, and Reading Football Club. Accommodation is in 38 en suite bedrooms, each with modern facilities.

The Farmhouse Inn Lodge
Burrfields Road, Portsmouth, Hampshire PO3 5HH
Tel: 023 92650510 • www.farmhouseinnlodge-portsmouth.co.uk

Five miles from Goodwood Racecourse and Portsmouth's historic Dockyard, this is an ideal place to relax - and best of all – play, with an 18-hole golf course and driving range nearby. Guests can dine in the lounge or outside on the patio. Two honeymoon suites and 74 other rooms are available, as well as executive and leisure suites.

THE GROSVENOR HOTEL
23 High Street, Stockbridge, Hampshire SO20 6EU
Tel: 01264 810 606 • www.grosvenorhotel-stockbridge.co.uk

This Georgian-style hotel is situated between the cathedral cities of Winchester and Salisbury. Dishes featuring local produce such as the chef's speciality Test Trout are on the menu in The Tom Cannon Restaurant. The wood panelled Bankside Bar also offers an à la carte menu and a range of snacks. A new wing provides accommodation with modern facilities.

Rates
S – SINGLE ROOM rate   D – Sharing DOUBLE/TWIN ROOM

S£ D£ = Under £35   S££ D££ = £36-£45   S£££ D£££ = £46-£55   S££££ D££££ = Over £55

This is meant as an indication only and does not show prices for Special Breaks, Weekends, etc. Guests are therefore advised to verify all prices on enquiring or booking.

THE THREE LIONS (on facing page)

7 BEDROOMS, ALL WITH PRIVATE BATHROOM. FREE HOUSE WITH REAL ALE. CHILDREN AND PETS WELCOME. RESTAURANT MEALS.
FORDINGBRIDGE 1 MILE. S££££, D£££

Isle of Wight

The 250 year old coaching inn, with new play area for 2011, will appeal to those looking for a traditional family-friendly pub.

• 2009 UK East of England Family Pub of the Year

- New Crazy Golf
- Food served all day
- Local Produce
- Local Ales
- Children's Play Area
- Beer Garden

Main Road • Ningwood • Isle of Wight • PO30 4NW
Tel: 01983 760672 • e-mail: info@horse-and-groom.com
www.horse-and-groom.com

NO ACCOMMODATION. FREE HOUSE WITH REAL ALE.
CHILDREN WELCOME. BAR AND RESTAURANT MEALS.
YARMOUTH 3 MILES.

Visit the FHG website
www.holidayguides.com
for details of the wide choice of accommodation featured in the full range of FHG titles

Isle of Wight

THE BOAT HOUSE
PUB · DINING · ROOMS

SPRINGVALE ROAD · SEAVIEW · ISLE OF WIGHT · PO34 5AW

Quality dining by the sea.

Now open under new ownership with an exciting new menu, real ales and an extensive wine selection.
Come and experience a new ambience with attentive service.
We have four newly refurbished en suite rooms, each tastefully furnished to provide a relaxing break by the sea.

Tel: 01983 810616 • email: info@theboathouseiow.co.uk
www.theboathouseiow.co.uk

4 BEDROOMS, ALL WITH PRIVATE BATHROOM. ALL BEDROOMS NON-SMOKING. FREE HOUSE WITH REAL ALE. CHILDREN WELCOME. BAR AND RESTAURANT MEALS.
RYDE 2 MILES. S££, D££££.

The Fountain Inn
High Street, Cowes, Isle of Wight PO31 7AW
Tel: 01983 292 397 • 01983 299 554 • www.fountaininn-cowes.co.uk

This Isle of Wight 'must-see' is famous in yachting circles as home to the Royal Yacht Club. It offers panoramic views of the harbour and shoreline, an early-bird buffet breakfast and a famous 'kilo of mussels' dinner. 20 en suite rooms all have direct-dial telephone, TV, hairdryer, trouser press and CD player.

Ryde Castle
Esplanade, Ryde, Isle of Wight PO33 1JA
Tel: 01983 563 755 • Fax: 01983 566 906 • www.rydecastle-hotel.co.uk

Visiting the Ryde Castle is like diving into a history textbook. This regal looking establishment has been a hospital and army HQ during both World Wars. Indulge in a pre-dinner drink and then dine in style in the brasserie. 18 en suite bedrooms have all modern facilities. Blackgang Chine and Fantasy Theme Park are nearby.

Isle of Wight — AA Pick of the Pubs 2005 - 2010

THE NEW INN
SHALFLEET, ISLE OF WIGHT

The New Inn is an Historic Inn dating from 1743, with inglenook fireplaces, flagstone floors, original low beamed ceilings and bags of character. The New Inn has a fine reputation for its culinary offerings, and due to its location at the foot of Newtown Estuary, fish dishes have become its speciality and The New Inn enjoys many accreditations.

Food served daily 12noon - 2.30pm and 6 - 9.30pm
(booking essential during peak times)

Tel 01983 531314 • info@thenew-inn.co.uk • www.thenew-inn.co.uk

NO ACCOMMODATION. FREE HOUSE WITH REAL ALE. CHILDREN WELCOME. PETS ALLOWED IN SOME AREAS. BAR AND RESTAURANT MEALS. YARMOUTH 4 MILES.

All kinds of watersports are available along the coast, but of course the Isle of Wight, only a short ferry ride away from the mainland, is the ultimate destination, with award-winning beaches, water sports centres, seakayaking, diving, sailing and windsurfing. For land-based activities there are over 500 miles of interconnected footpaths, historic castles, dinosaur museums, theme parks and activity centres, while the resorts like Sandown, Shanklin, Ryde and Ventnor offer all that is associated with a traditional seaside holiday. There is a thriving arts community, and of course two internationally renowned music festivals held every year. Something for everyone!

HolidayGuides.com
visit our website for details of hundreds of properties throughout Britain

LONDON & SOUTH EAST ENGLAND   Kent 55

Kent

COCK INN
Boughton Monchelsea, Maidstone ME17 4JD
- Tel: 01622 743166
- www.cockinnboughtonmonchelsea.com
- e-mail: info@cockinnboughtonmonchelsea.com
- Glorious 16thC timbered black and white inn.
- Patio and outside eating area.
- Inglenook fireplace and oak-beamed bar and restaurant.
- Freshly prepared country cuisine using seasonal produce.
- Selection of real ales along with a choice of fine wines.

NO ACCOMMODATION. REAL ALE.
CHILDREN AND PETS WELCOME. BAR AND RESTAURANT MEALS.
MAIDSTONE 3 MILES.

The Flagship
115 Snargate Sreet, Dover, Kent CT17 9DA
Tel: 01322 862087

A stylish Kentish establishment offering menu classics such as seafood and mature steaks, plus carefully selected wines, guest beers and real ales. Parking available.

Kings Arms Hotel
Market Square, Westerham, Kent TN16 1AN
Tel: 01959 562 990 • Fax: 01959 561 240 • www.kingsarms-westerham-kent.co.uk

Take full advantage of the sales at Blue Water Shopping Centre, which is located only 20 minutes away. Enjoy some chilled entertainment over a light lunch or early evening tipple in The Conservatory, light and airy for summer relaxation. All rooms are en suite, with satellite TV and music centre.

Family-Friendly Pubs, Inns & Hotels
See the Supplement on pages 177-178
for establishments which really welcome children

Oxfordshire

LONDON & SOUTH EAST ENGLAND

The Inn for All Seasons is an unspoilt former C16 Coaching Inn just off the A40, 3 miles west of Burford in the heart of the Cotswolds. It's a traditional family-run Inn that has 10 comfortable en suite rooms including a four-poster. It's been in the Sharp family for two generations.

We serve great food, locally sourced where possible with fabulous fresh fish a speciality. Combine this with traditional cask and local ales, a well stocked wine cellar, log fires, flagstone floors, wooden beams and leather wing back chairs – it's all you need to relax and unwind. Matthew and Heather look forward to welcoming you.

The Barringtons, Near Burford, Oxfordshire OX18 4TN • Tel: 01451 844324
email: info@innforallseasons.com • www.innforallseasons.co.uk
B&B from £45.00* • Dinner, B&B from £74.00*
(*pppn, on a twin/double sharing basis)

10 BEDROOMS, ALL WITH PRIVATE BATHROOM. ALL BEDROOMS NON-SMOKING. PETS WELCOME.
BAR AND RESTAURANT MEALS.
BURFORD 3 MILES. S£££, D££££.

Rates

S – SINGLE ROOM rate   D – Sharing DOUBLE/TWIN ROOM

S£ D£ = Under £35   S££ D££ = £36-£45   S£££ D£££ = £46-£55   S££££ D££££ = Over £55

This is meant as an indication only and does not show prices for Special Breaks, Weekends, etc.
Guests are therefore advised to verify all prices on enquiring or booking.

Surrey

Chase Lodge House

In Autumn 2010, Sky TV described Chase Lodge as "The best kept secret in West London". This small, romantic and independent hotel is just half an hour from Heathrow Airport and Central London. Hampton Court Palace, the River Thames and Bushy Park are just a stone's throw away. There are many excellent restaurants nearby, including Jamie's Italian, Carluccio's and Simply Thai, which won Best Local Thai on Gordon Ramsay's *F-Word*.

Each room at Chase Lodge is unique, and has a flatscreen TV and free Wi-Fi.

The hotel is dog-friendly, and we recently accommodated the dogs from the BBC TV series *"Over the Rainbow"*.

Parking is free between 4pm and 10am; there is an £8 charge during the day.

"A hidden gem".

Rates: Single room from £49, double from £69.
Price includes VAT and Continental breakfast.

Chase Lodge House
10 Park Road, Hampton Wick, Kingston upon Thames KY1 4AS
Tel: 020 8943 1862 • Fax: 020 8943 9363
e-mail: info@chaselodgehotel.com • www.chaselodgehotel.com

Readers are requested to mention this FHG guide when seeking accommodation

---

THE COMPASSES INN *(on next page)*

2 BEDROOMS, ALL WITH PRIVATE BATHROOM. REAL ALES. CHILDREN WELCOME, PETS ALLOWED IN BAR ONLY. BAR AND RESTAURANT MEALS.
GUILDFORD 6 MILES. ££££ PER ROOM PER NIGHT.

The COMPASSES Inn
Purveyors of fine food, ale and .....music!

This attractive inn was once known as the 'God Encompasses' but through time and mispronunciation is now simply known as the 'Compasses'.

Known for its appetising selection of home-cooked dishes and supporting local Surrey Hills Brewery, this friendly hostelry has a warm ambience accentuated by its exposed oak beams and horse brasses. There is good traditional home-cooked food in the bar and the restaurant. and live music every Friday. Situated beneath the North Downs, there is a popular beer garden through which runs the Tilling Bourne Stream.

THE RESTAURANT

The restaurant is accessed from the main bar or directly from the road side entrance.
Open all day we serve food from 12pm – 9pm.
Full bar menu, Chef's daily specials board.
All of our food is home cooked to order and served with fresh vegetables.
Individual or special dietary needs can easily be catered for.
A la carte menu is served in our non-smoking restaurant from Wednesday to Saturday evenings.
We can cater for any size party whether it is an intimate dinner for two or a private function for two hundred. Our chefs will create a menu to suit you.

THE BAR

The main bar is accessed directly from the car park. This room is adorned with implements connected with local history such as farming, and adds further to the character and charm of The Compasses.
There is ample seating and standing area.
The bar prides itself in keeping a fine stock of wines and spirits and is noteworthy amongst connoisseurs for real ales.
Our most noteworthy supplier of fine ales is the **Surrey Hills Brewery.**

THE FESTIVAL

In recent years The Compasses has been responsible for organising a mini festival now known as 'Gomstock'.
Weather permitting, the festival is set within the delightful surroundings of The Compasses garden with green lawns rolling down to the gently flowing Tilling Bourne brook.
The event features musicians and other entertainment activities for all age groups, hence 'Gomstock'. It has now become a favourite family event which attracts both locals and visitors from much further afield. The proceeds of this event are distributed to charities.
All guests invited to perform such as the musicians kindly give their services completely free of charge. The event usually takes place during the August Bank Holiday weekend.

**Station Road, Gomshall,
Surrey GU5 9LA
Tel: 01483 202 506
www.thecompassesinn.co.uk**

East Sussex

The George Inn

Relax • Indulge • Explore • Welcome

High Street, Alfriston, East Sussex BN26 5SY

With delicious food, sumptuous relaxing bedrooms, refreshing ales, oak beams, open log fires, friendly atmosphere, quality service and a beautiful location, we have all you need to fully enjoy your time at the 14th Century George Inn, Alfriston.
Six beautiful and luxurious bedrooms with oak beams, bespoke antique furniture and sleigh beds.
All en suite, all with showers, and four with baths.
Hearty lunches, candlelit evening meals, excellent wine list and great selection of real ales. The surrounding area is steeped in history and wonderful countryside and just waiting to be explored and discovered!

Telephone: 01323 870319 • Fax: 01323 871384
E-mail: info@thegeorge-alfriston.com
www.thegeorge-alfriston.com

6 BEDROOMS, ALL WITH PRIVATE BATHROOM. ALL BEDROOMS NON-SMOKING. REAL ALE.
CHILDREN WELCOME. BAR AND RESTAURANT MEALS.
NEWHAVEN 4 MILES. S££££, D££££.

The Green Man

Lewes Road, Ringmer, East Sussex BN8 5NA
Tel: 01273 812422 • www.greenmanringmer.co.uk

The new decked patio area makes outdoor dining a real treat here at the Green Man in Ringmer. The restaurant has a reputation for good service and even better food - the Sunday Carvery is especially popular and is a great excuse for a family day out. The bar is stocked with a varied selection of beers, lagers, real ales and fine wines.

The Buccaneer
10 Compton Street, Eastbourne, East Sussex BN21 4BW • Tel: 01323 732 829

Located in the heart of theatreland and popular with patrons for a pre- or post-theatre tipple, this majestic building was built in the style of the Pavilion at Brighton. It offers a good selection of hand-pulled real ales and other refreshments. Pub food is served every day from a varied menu, and Sunday lunch is particularly popular.

The Farm@Friday Street
Friday Street, Langney, Eastbourne, East Sussex BN23 8AP
Tel: 01323 766049 • www.farmfridaystreet.com

After an extensive refurbishment, oak beams, stone-flagged floors, authentic log fires and leather sofas create a welcoming pub atmosphere. Food and drink is reasonably priced, with the emphasis on fresh local produce wherever possible.

THE WHEEL INN
Heathfield Road, Burwash Weald, Etchingham, East Sussex TN19 7LA
Tel: 01435 882758 • Fax: 01435 883625

The Wheel Inn is situated in an area of outstanding natural beauty and offers a good choice of lagers, beers, spirits and mixers. This free house stocks its own British cask conditioned real ales. Facilities include a pool table and dart board.

The Swan Mountain
Lewes Road, Forest Row, East Sussex RH18 5ER • Tel: 01342 822318

The Swan Mountain is well worth seeking out. The interior is very cosy, with open log fires, low-beamed ceilings and a snug – all the traditional features one hopes to find in a friendly family pub. Other delightful features include a restaurant area and a sun terrace for outdoor dining in summer months.

The Roebuck
Wych Cross, Forest Row, East Sussex RH18 5JL
Tel: 01342 823 811 • www.roebuckhotel-gatwick.co.uk

Winnie the Pooh fans may remember hearing about Forest Row as it borders Royal Ashdown Forest, where the famous bear lived! Summers are delightful at the Roebuck with its outdoor patio and restaurants. Accommodation is in 30 en suite bedrooms, all with modern facilities. Brighton and Royal Tunbridge Wells are a short drive away.

The White Hart
Winchelsea Road, Guestling, Near Hastings, East Sussex TN35 4LW
Tel: 01424 813187

The White Hart is a Beefeater pub in an Grade II Listed building with a country house atmosphere. Log fires and traditional furnishings and fittings create a charming olde worlde ambience, and the bar is stocked with a good variety of beers, lagers, ales and fine wines. Children are welcome at this establishment, and there is a large beer garden.

The Old Ship Inn

A traditional family-run 17th century Country Inn. The perfect place to relax and enjoy home-made food and traditional ales.
Food served from 12 to 9.30 pm daily. The charming oak-beamed bar and restaurant is set in one acre of well tended, enclosed gardens.
Children are welcome and have their own menu.
Special events can be catered for from birthdays to prize giving.
You find us on the A26 between Lewes and Uckfield.
Well behaved dogs welcome inside.

Uckfield Road, Ringmer
East Sussex BN8 5RP
Tel: 01273 814223
e-mail: info@oldshippub.co.uk   www.oldshippub.co.uk

NO ACCOMMODATION. FREE HOUSE WITH REAL ALE.
CHILDREN AND PETS WELCOME. BAR AND RESTAURANT MEALS.
BRIGHTON 11 MILES.

The Druid's Head
9 Brighton Place, Brighton, East Sussex BN1 1HJ
Tel: 01273 325490

A popular Sussex Coast pub and diner with an unpretentious atmosphere. Some of the outside brickwork dates all the way back to 1510, with sash windows and other period features. The cuisine is varied and of a very high standard, and beers and ales are well kept.

The Franklin Tavern
158 Lewes Road, Brighton, East Sussex BN2 3LF
Tel: 01273 602995 • Fax: 01273 698535

The pub is close to Brighton University and is popular with family and friends visiting students. Food and drinks are reasonably priced, and live sporting fixtures are shown on large plasma screens.

West Sussex

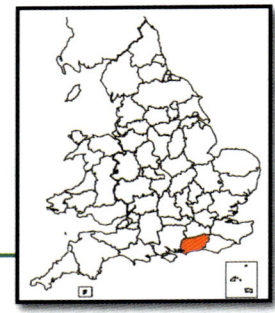

The HALFWAY BRIDGE
PETWORTH

With the South Downs as a backdrop, Paul and Sue Carter welcome you to their fabulous retreat in the heart of classic Polo country.

Bar, Restaurant & Luxury Rooms

www.thesussexpub.co.uk
For reservations and enquiries ring
01798 861281
Halfway Bridge, Petworth
West Sussex GU28 9BP

6 BEDROOMS/SUITES, ALL WITH PRIVATE BATHROOM. CHILDREN AND PETS WELCOME.
BAR LUNCHES AND RESTAURANT MEALS.
CHICHESTER 13 MILES.

FISH HOUSE (on facing page)

15 BEDROOMS, ALL WITH PRIVATE BATHROOM. ALL BEDROOMS NON-SMOKING.
PETS WELCOME. BAR AND RESTAURANT MEALS.
CHICHESTER 8 MILES.

local • organic • scrumptious

Discover the Fish House...

- The Fish House has redefined culinary excellence across the south, and brought luxurious overnight accommodation to the rolling Sussex countryside.
- The venue provides an oasis of sumptuous dining, and self-indulgent relaxation, on the outskirts of Chichester and close to Goodwood.
- Experience the atmospheric Fish Bar, with its show-stopping Oyster counter and sample the seafood delights. A mouth-watering menu offers classics and international dishes, all from organic sources.
- In the restaurant guests can experience the finest in à la carte dining. Chef Alan Gleeson brings with him a passion for sourcing and preparing the freshest seafood and the finest local organic produce.
- Fifteen luxurious guest rooms, each named after a famous fishing port, succeed in marrying the latest technology with chic interior furnishing. No corners have been cut in creating luxurious accommodation you just won't wish to leave.
- Seven secluded hot tubs are set in landscaped grounds, each with its own private thatched gazebo, the ultimate in post-dining luxury. Book early to avoid disappointment.
- The large, landscaped grounds present outdoor seating for in excess of 120 covers, making The Fish House the ideal venue for private events, weddings and parties.

Luxury Hotel Accommodation and Restaurant

The Fish House • Chilgrove • Chichester • West Sussex PO18 9HX
Tel 01243 519 444 • Fax 01243 519 499
reservations: bookings@thefishhouse.co.uk
www.thefishhouse.co.uk

Bedfordshire

The Bull
259 London Road, Bedford, Bedfordshire MK42 0PX
Tel: 01234 355719

The Bull with its mock Tudor exterior offers an extensive selection of weekly activities, including a quiz night, pool tournament, and Thursday night curry club. With a wide range of pub snacks, food deals and drinks offers, wifi, and live sport on plasma screens, there is something for everyone. Children and dogs are welcome in the outdoor area.

The Castle
Newham Street, Bedford, Bedfordshire MK40 3JR • Tel: 01234 353295
www.thecastlepubbedford.co.uk

Located in a popular area of Bedford, The Castle dates back 200 years, and is a perfect place for post-work get-togethers over an ale or fine wine. Home-made, hearty meals are of great value and size, and B&B accommodation is available in one single and three twin rooms.

The Pheasant
300 Kimbolton Road, Bedford, Bedfordshire MK41 8YR
Tel: 01234 409301

A Bedfordshire pub for all the family, with live sport shown on two large-screen TVs, a children's play area, pool table and dart board. The lunchtime menu offers freshly prepared pub favourites accompanied by teas, coffees, real ales and fine wines. In summer months the beer garden is popular with locals and visitors alike.

THE GLOBE INN (on facing page)

NO ACCOMMODATION. GREENE KING HOUSE WITH REAL ALE. CHILDREN WELCOME. BAR AND RESTAURANT MEALS.
LUTON 11 MILES.

- ★ Canal-side location with access over own bridge.
- ★ Beer garden with outdoor eating facilities
- ★ Bar/Lounge open all day, every day
- ★ Children welcome
- ★ Brand new children's play equipment with slide
- ★ Dogs welcome in bar area
- ★ Excellent choice of food served 12 noon-10pm daily
- ★ Cask Marque Accredited 2010
- ★ Booking Highly Recommended

THE Globe INN

Globe Lane, Stoke Road, Old Linslade, Leighton Buzzard, Bedfordshire LU7 2TA
Tel: 01525 373338
www.globeinn-leighton-buzzard.co.uk
e-mail: 6458@greeneking.co.uk

NOW ON FACEBOOK become a fan!

Cambridgeshire

THE ANCHOR INN
Sutton Gault, Near Ely, Cambridgeshire CB6 2BD

The 17th Century Anchor Inn offers modern British cuisine with an emphasis on seasonal and traditional ingredients; superb wine list. We have four guest bedrooms offering a variety of accommodation to suit every need.
The Anchor is ideally situated for exploring East Anglia; it is only 7 miles from Ely and is less than half an hour from Cambridge. Newmarket and its racecourse are within easy reach.

Tel: 01353 778537
Fax: 01353 776180
e-mail: anchorinn@popmail.bta.com
www.anchor-inn-restaurant.co.uk

4 BEDROOMS, ALL WITH PRIVATE BATHROOM. ALL BEDROOMS NON-SMOKING. FREE HOUSE WITH REAL ALE. CHILDREN WELCOME.
ELY 6 MILES. S££££, D££.

Rates
S – SINGLE ROOM rate   D – Sharing DOUBLE/TWIN ROOM

S£ D£ = Under £35   S££ D££ = £36-£45   S£££ D£££ = £46-£55   S££££ D££££ = Over £55

This is meant as an indication only and does not show prices for Special Breaks, Weekends, etc. Guests are therefore advised to verify all prices on enquiring or booking.

The Boathouse
14 Chesterton Road, Cambridge, Cambridgeshire CB4 3AX • Tel: 01223 460905

Pleasant, waterside establishment set in beautiful Cambridgeshire surroundings, serving real ales, Continental lagers, soft drinks and Costa coffee. Amenities include a games room, plasma screen TVs, a pool table, beer garden, and a varied food menu offering English, Thai, Mexican and Italian cuisine.

The Fox
Gladeside Bar Hill, Cambridge, Cambridgeshire CB3 8DY • Tel: 01954 780305

Bar Hill's pride and joy – a stylish, well maintained venue with a sociable layout. Children are welcome, and amenities include an outdoor children's play area, pool table and jukebox.

The George
High Street, Spaldwick, Huntingdon, Cambridgeshire PE28 0TD • Tel: 01480 890293
www.georgeofspaldwick.co.uk

This pub's high street setting means that it is a firm favourite with locals as well as passers by. The mixture of olde world and contemporary is well balanced, and the restaurant has a great reputation, with a choice of Mediterranean, New World and English cuisine.

The Waggon & Horses
39 High Street, Milton, Cambridgeshire CB4 6DF • Tel: 01223 860313

Listed in *The Good Beer Guide* is this prominent mock-Tudor style venue with an interesting preoccupation with hats and pictures - and an impressive collection of both! In the beer garden are swings, a slide and chickens too! Regular features include bar billiards, a quiz night, balti night, a dart board and piano.

Palmerston Arms
82 Oundle Road, Peterborough, Cambridgeshire PE2 9PA
Tel: 01733 565865 • www.palmerston-arms.co.uk

'The Palmy' is an olde world pub steeped in traditional pub values. Behind the bar is a selection of good quality real ales, draught ciders and perry, direct from the cask. When hunger strikes, try a Cornish pasty or freshly made pie.

Please mention **Pubs & Inns of Britain** when making enquiries about accommodation featured in these pages

THE WOODMAN
Thorpe Wood, Peterborough, Cambridgeshire PE3 6SQ • Tel: 01733 267601

Situated in the Longthorpe area is this golfing themed inn, furnished with suede and leather seats and sofas. Early breakfast is available for dedicated golfers and the regular food menu is available from noon onwards. Wifi access, TV, pool table, large beer garden and patio area.

The Harrier
184 Gunthorpe Road, Peterborough, Cambridgeshire PE4 7DS
Tel: 01733 575362 • Fax: 01733 575364

A modern family pub, a member of the Hungry Horse group, where the menu is a major attraction. The staff are particularly helpful and work tirelessly behind the well stocked bar. Facilities include a pool table, big screen TV and decked chill-out area for adults.

The Halcyon
Atherstone Avenue, Peterborough, Cambridgeshire PE3 9TT
Tel: 01733 263801 • www.woodman-pub-peterborough.co.uk

After an extensive makeover, The Halcyon offers a Hungry Horse food menu – affordable and varied! Regular activities include live bands and a poker night, and there is a dart board, pool table and a smoking shelter with TV installed!

Milton Arms
205 Milton Road, Cambridge, Cambridgeshire CB4 1XG • Tel: 01223 505012

Situated in a residential area north of Cambridge, the Milton Arms is a member of the Hungry Horse hospitality scheme, with a large dining area and a peaceful lounge area with comfy furniture. Amenities include wifi access, a new outdoor children's play area, a sports bar with a pool table, flat screen TVs, and a beer garden and alfresco dining area.

The Red Lion
33 High Street, Grantchester, Cambridgeshire CB3 9NF • Tel: 01223 840121
www.redlion-grantchester.co.uk

Traditional, thatched pub located in an idyllic area by the river in Grantchester; a path in the garden leads to the tranquil River Cam. The first-class menu offers seafood and game dishes, plus a vegetarian option, and there is also a children's menu.

HolidayGuides.com
visit our website for details of hundreds of properties throughout Britain

EAST OF ENGLAND

Essex

- Bed & Breakfast accommodation on the Essex Way • Lovely double and twin rooms - all en suite • Free Wi-Fi • Traditional home cooked food • A la carte evening menu, all freshly prepared to order • Friendly and relaxed cosy atmosphere • Sunday Lunch - booking advisable

Chatham Green,
Near Little Waltham,
Chelmsford CM3 3LE
Tel: 01245 361188

enquiries@windmillmotorinn.co.uk
www.windmillmotorinn.co.uk

THE WINDMILL INN
Accommodation, Restaurant & Bar

7 BEDROOMS, ALL WITH PRIVATE BATHROOM. ALL BEDROOMS NON-SMOKING. FREE HOUSE WITH REAL ALE. CHILDREN AND PETS WELCOME. BAR AND RESTAURANT MEALS. CHELMSFORD 4 MILES. D£££token£.

The Lion & Lamb
Stortford Road, Little Canfield, Near Takeley, Dunmow, Essex CM6 1SR
Tel: 01279 870257 • Fax: 01279 870523 • www.lionandlamb.co.uk

Bar and restaurant providing customers with the perfect setting for that romantic evening for two, or a long awaited catch-up drink with friends. Tradition prevails when it comes to decor, with blackened oak beams, a huge open fire and soft lighting.

The Whalebone Freehouse

http://whaleboneinn.sm4.biz

Chapel Road, Fingringhoe,
Colchester, Essex CO5 7BG

Tel/Fax: 01206 729307 • vicki@thewhaleboneinn.co.uk

The Whalebone offers a wide range of excellent food and real ales. This Grade II Listed building is set in the heart of the Roman River Valley. Only minutes from Colchester, Fingrinhoe Nature Reserve and within walking distance of the foot ferry (summer only) across the River Colne. Corporate, office and large parties catered for in the great atmosphere of the Barn Function Room.

NO ACCOMMODATION. FREE HOUSE WITH REAL ALE.
BAR AND RESTAURANT MEALS.
COLCHESTER 4 MILES.

The Bull Hotel

Bridge Street, Halstead, Essex, CO9 1HU
Tel: 01787 472144 • 01787 472496 • www.bullhotel-halstead.co.uk

The Bull is a lively and very popular high street pub/inn, suitable for just about every occasion. Whether you're looking for a stopover, some live music or a beautiful garden to dine 'al fresco' in the summer months, look no further. All 16 rooms are en suite, with colour TV and coffee/tea making facilities.

From the historic port of Harwich in the north to the Thames estuary in the south, the 300 miles of coastline and dry climate of maritime Essex have attracted holiday makers since early Victorian times. There are fun family resorts with plenty of action like Clacton, on the Essex sunshine coast, and Southend-on-Sea, with over six miles of clean safe sand and the world's longest pleasure pier. Along the coast there are quiet clifftop walks, sheltered coves, long beaches, mudflats, saltmarshes and creeks. Previously the haunt of smugglers, these are now a great attraction for birdwatchers, particularly for viewing winter wildfowl. At Maldon take a trip on a Thames barge to see the seal colonies or cross the Saxon causeway to Mersea Island to taste the oysters, washed down by wine produced on the vineyard there, but watch the tides! Yachting is a favourite pastime at Burnham-on-Crouch, but for land-based transport visit the railway museum with working locomotives. Walkers and cyclists will enjoy the gently rolling landscape of the Essex countryside. Keen gardeners can visit the restored and preserved gardens at Audley End, Easton Lodge and Hylands House or the contemporary designs of Beth Chatto's gravel, water and woodland gardens near Colchester and Sir Frederick Gibberd's garden near Harlow. Explore the medieval towns and villages like Thaxted and Saffron Walden, where long ago saffron was produced for the textile industry, the Norman keep at Colchester, England's oldest town and the grand stately homes like Ingatestone Hall and Audley End. All this within an hour of London!

EAST OF ENGLAND   Hertfordshire

Hertfordshire

Ye Olde Mitre Inn
58 High Street, Barnet, Hertfordshire EN5 5SJ
Tel: 020 8449 6582 • www.pub-explorer.com/herts/pub/mitrebarnet.htm
This dog-friendly (on leads!) pub is positioned on Barnet's popular and busy high street. The bar stocks a wide range of draught beers, real ales and cocktails (to order), all of which can be enjoyed in the bar, living area or restaurant.

The Duke Of York
Ganwick Corner, Barnet Road, Barnet, Hertfordshire EN5 4SG
Tel: 0208 4490297 • www.pub-explorer.com/herts/pub/dukeofyorkbarnet.htm
Superbly refurbished gastro bar and dining room, with easy access to Barnet High Street and Arkley countryside. It offers draught beers and regularly changing guest ales at the bar, and an imaginative menu in the restaurant.

THE SUN HOTEL
Sun Street, Hitchin, Hertfordshire SG5 1AF
Tel: 01462 432 092 • Fax: 01462 431 488 • www.sunhotel-hitchin.com
The Sun, with its delightful interior, is situated in Hitchin and dates back to the 16th century. Enjoy an excellent meal in the hotel's restaurant, which features dishes from around the world as well as traditional English cuisine. Real ales and fine wines are also available. 32 en suite bedrooms have wifi, CD player and colour TV.

The Valiant Trooper
Trooper Road, Aldbury, Tring, Hertfordshire HP23 5RW
Tel: 01442 851203 • www.valianttrooper.co.uk/
This Valiant Trooper offers many traditional feaures such as beamed ceilings, an inglenook fireplace, exposed brickwork, and a woodburning stove. The converted barn at the rear (now a restaurant) completes this beautifully positioned establishment.

Norfolk

The Feathers Hotel

Manor Road, Dersingham, King's Lynn, Norfolk PE31 6LN
Tel & Fax: 01485 540207

In the gently undulating countryside of north-west Norfolk, this solid and welcoming stone-built inn stands on the fringe of Sandringham Estate, one of the Queen's favourite country homes. While not claiming to compete with that offered to Her Majesty, the Feathers provides comfortable and reasonably priced en suite accommodation with bedrooms simply furnished in the modern style and each having colour television. Real ale is served in the two popular bars, the Saddle Room and the Sandringham, and a right royal cuisine is provided with both à la carte and table d'hôte menus available. Well-tended gardens make a most pleasant setting for this attractive hostelry.

e-mail: info@thefeathershotelnorfolk.co.uk
www.thefeathershotelnorfolk.co.uk

ALL ROOMS WITH PRIVATE BATHROOM. REAL ALE. CHILDREN WELCOME.
BAR AND RESTAURANT MEALS.
HUNSTANTON 7 MILES. S££££, D££££.

Rates

S – SINGLE ROOM rate   D – Sharing DOUBLE/TWIN ROOM

S£ D£ = Under £35   S££ D££ = £36-£45   S£££ D£££ = £46-£55   S££££ D££££ = Over £55

This is meant as an indication only and does not show prices for Special Breaks, Weekends, etc.
Guests are therefore advised to verify all prices on enquiring or booking.

EAST OF ENGLAND
Norfolk

THE Hill House
Happisburgh NR12 0PW
Tel & Fax: 01692 650004

This attractive free house on the lonely Norfolk coast at Happisburgh (pronounced 'Hazeborough') was once the favourite haunt of the remarkable Sir Arthur Conan Doyle, creator of Sherlock Holmes. Clues may be found in that the coastline here is renowned for its ghosts and has been a graveyard for ships over the years which have foundered on the formidable Haisborough Sands, some seven miles off-shore. However, conviviality and good fare is provided by a visit to the inn's beamed bar and restaurant.

Excellent accommodation is available in spacious rooms and there is a large garden in which a double en suite room has been created in a converted signal box overlooking the sea. Different!

4 BEDROOMS, 2 WITH PRIVATE BATHROOM. FREE HOUSE WITH REAL ALE. CHILDREN AND PETS WELCOME. BAR MEALS LUNCHTIME AND EVENINGS, RESTAURANT MENU EVENINGS ONLY. NON-SMOKING AREAS. WALSHAM 6 MILES. S£, D£

The Bull
25 High Street, Dereham, Norfolk NR19 1DZ • Tel: 01362 697771

Situated in the town centre on the main High Street is this Listed pub, with open fires and original oak beams. The Bull is an ideal lunchtime retreat, with reasonably priced food and facilities including plasma screens, a pool table and dart board.

The Otter
12 The Square, Thorpe Marriot, Drayton, Norfolk NR8 6XE • Tel: 01603 260455

Located just a short distance from Norwich, this fully refurbished family pub has an open-plan layout, where patrons can enjoy a delicious meal from the Sizzler menu. Live sporting fixtures are shown on screens in the sports bar downstairs. Free wifi access throughout.

The Lifeboat Inn

16th Century Smugglers' Ale House

Ship Lane, Thornham, Norfolk PE36 6LT
Tel: 01485 512236 • Fax: 01485 512323
e-mail: lifeboatinn@maypolehotels.com

THE LIFEBOAT INN has been a welcome sight for the weary traveller for centuries – roaring open fires, real ales and a hearty meal awaiting. The Summer brings its own charm – a cool beer, gazing over open meadows to the harbour, and rolling white horses gently breaking upon Thornham's sandy beach.

Dogs are welcome in all our bars and we provide the sort of breakfast that will enable you to keep up with your four-legged friend on the way to the beach!

Guests arriving at reception are greeted by our grand old fireplace in the lounge – ideal for toasting your feet after a day walking the coastal path – if you can coax your sleeping dog out of prime position! The restaurant (AA Rosette) opens every evening offering a varied selection of dishes to suit all tastes. Our extensive bar snack menu is also available if guests wish their pets to join them in the bar.

There are numerous and varied walks along miles of open beaches, across sweeping sand dunes, through pine woods or along chalk and sandstone cliff tops. It is truly a walker's paradise – especially if you're a dog.

We hope you will come and visit us. For our brochure and tariff which includes details of breaks please ring 01485 512336 or visit our website

www.maypolehotels.com

14 BEDROOMS, ALL WITH PRIVATE BATHROOM.
PETS WELCOME. BAR AND RESTAURANT MEALS.
HUNSTANTON 4 MILES.

The Rushcutters Arms
Thorpe-St-Andrew, Norwich, Norfolk NR7 0HE
Tel.: 01603 435403 • Fax: 01603 439790

On the outskirts of Norwich in the peaceful village of Thorpe St Andrew, this Grade II Listed venue offers guests a traditional pub experience, with open fires, large oak beams and charming alcoves, nooks and crannies. The food is popular here and prepared from fresh ingredients. Facilities include an outdoor patio overlooking the Norfolk Broads.

THE WHEATSHEAF
Church Road, West Beckham, Near Holt, Norfolk NR25 6NX
Tel: 01263 822110

This beautiful pub is steeped in history and situated in West Beckham, near Holt. Inside, there are two separate dining rooms and a beamed bar area with a log fire. The food is home cooked, with a range of dishes from light snacks to main meals. Self-catering accommodation is available all year round.

www.holidayguides.com

EAST OF ENGLAND
Norfolk

Fishermans Return

This 300-year-old brick and flint pub is situated in the unspoilt village of Winterton-on-Sea, just a few minutes' stroll from sandy beaches and beautiful walks. The Inn is popular with locals and visitors alike, serving excellent food, from simple bar snacks to more substantial fare, with a good choice of local real ales and fine wines. Accommodation is available on a B&B basis, in three tastefully furnished en suite double bedrooms.

The Lane, Winterton-on-Sea NR29 4BN
Tel: 01493 393305
e-mail: fishermansreturn@yahoo.co.uk
www.fishermans-return.com

3 ROOMS, ALL WITH PRIVATE BATHROOM. FREE HOUSE WITH REAL ALE. BAR MEALS. GREAT YARMOUTH 8 MILES.

The Banningham Crown
Church Road, Banningham, Norwich, Norfolk NR11 7DY
Tel: 01263 733534 • www.banninghamcrown.co.uk

Located opposite the village green in the quiet village of Banningham is this CAMRA listed pub and restaurant. It offers a full à la carte menu, bar snacks and a great selection of real ales. Entertainment includes live jazz nights, BBQs, Morris dancers and quiz nights.

THE BELL HOTEL
King Street, Thetford, Norfolk IP24 2AZ
Tel: 01842 754 455 • Fax: 01842 755 552 • www.bellinn-thetford.co.uk

Thetford, an old cathedral town, is a tranquil Norfolk getaway. The Bell featured regularly in the popular sitcom 'Dad's Army', playing second home to cast and crew. Standard rooms are en suite, with colour TV and coffee/tea making amenities; special feature rooms also available.

Suffolk

THE BROME GRANGE HOTEL
Norwich Road, Brome, Near Eye, Suffolk IP23 8AP
Tel: 01379 870456 • www.bromegrange.co.uk • bromegrange@fastnet.co.uk

Set amid the Suffolk countryside, The Grange boasts 22 ground floor en suite rooms, all with views of the beautiful hotel gardens. Single, double, twin or family size rooms are available. The stylish Knight's Restaurant serves à la carte international and English dishes with produce from the hotel's own organic free-range farm.

The Beehive
The Street, Horringer, Bury St Edmunds, Suffolk IP29 5SN • Tel: 01284 735260
www.beehivehorringer.co.uk

This beautiful pub boasts an award-winning restaurant serving fresh, home-made dishes prepared from local ingredients. The building has exposed flint walls, and inside is traditional in style, with a number of charming little nooks and crannies.

The Dog & Partridge
29 Crown Street, Bury St Edmunds, Suffolk IP33 1QU • Tel: 01284 764792

Put your overnight bag down at the adjacent inn and pop in to the pub next door for a nightcap. Drink and dine in peace, play some pool, watch the football highlights, or simply pull up a pew outside in either of the two courtyards. Accommodation is nine non-smoking bedrooms. Wifi hotspot available.

The Mill Inn
Market Cross Place, Aldeburgh, Suffolk IP15 5BJ
Tel: 01728 452363 • www.themillinnaldeburgh.com

On the sea front at Aldeburgh, this popular pub provides comfortable accommodation and easy access to the beach, as well as to shopping amenities, cinema and theatre. Drop in for a delicious bar snack or a glass of real ale. Rooms have colour TV, tea/coffee tray, and hairdryer.

EAST OF ENGLAND
Suffolk

The Bull Inn
Woolpit • Bury St Edmunds

The Bull Inn at Woolpit, near Bury St Edmunds, is a traditional Suffolk Country family-run Pub, offering a warm welcome, very comfortable accommodation and excellent service, together with good traditional food and ales and a fine selection of wines.

In the centre of a pretty village just off the A14 between Bury St. Edmunds and Stowmarket, The Bull Inn is within easy reach of all parts of this beautiful county, and offers an ideal base for touring East Anglia.

Whether you want to pop in for a quick drink, enjoy a leisurely lunch or dinner, or stay a while in one of the comfortable en suite bedrooms, you will be most welcome.

The Bull Inn offers a choice of accommodation, either singles, doubles or family rooms. All our rooms offer en suite facilities, tea/coffee making facilities and TV.

The Bull Inn & Restaurant
The Street, Woolpit, Bury St Edmunds IP30 9SA
Tel: 01359 240393 • e-mail: info@bullinnwoolpit.co.uk
www.bullinnwoolpit.co.uk

The Spread Eagle
Out Westgate, Bury St Edmunds, Suffolk IP33 2DE • Tel: 01284 754523

'A pub for all ages' is this establishment's slogan. Food is served throughout the week, with an unbeatable Sunday roast lunch as a highlight. Facilities include quiz nights with free buffets, three plasma screens and a children's play area.

The Ship Inn at Dunwich
St James Street, Dunwich, Suffolk IP17 3DT
Tel: 01728 648219 • www.shipatdunwich.co.uk

The Inn is positioned just a short drive away from neighbouring seaside towns, Southwold and Aldeburgh. Single, double and family rooms are available, each en suite, with coffee/tea making facilities and colour TV. The pub's dining room is renowned for its adventurous menu and helped gain the pub a rave review in *The Good Pub Guide*.

THE GROSVENOR
25/31 Ranelagh Road, Felixstowe, Suffolk IP11 7HA • Tel: 01394 284137

This authentic public house has retained most of its original features, and the interior includes comfortable lounges, a pool room and a bar area. Live sporting fixtures are shown on a large screen TV, with a jukebox and a dart board for patrons' enjoyment.

The Huntsman & Hound
Stone Street, Spexhall, Halesworth, Suffolk IP19 0RN • Tel: 01986 781341

Traditional 15th century Inn close to the Suffolk coast, with the Norfolk Broads just a short drive away. Stay in one of three bedrooms, each en suite, with colour TV and coffee/tea making facilities. Enjoy a pint of real ale in the bar area and some freshly home-cooked food. Pets welcome by arrangement.

The Thrasher
Nacton Road, Ipswich, Suffolk IP3 9RZ • Tel: 01473 723355

Having undergone a major refurbishment, the pub is now a focal point of the local community. The stylish interior is elegantly decorated, with impressive LCD TV screens in the restaurant's seating area. The cuisine is particularly popular, with something for everyone on the imaginative menu.

THE BULL INN (on previous page)

8 BEDROOMS, ALL WITH PRIVATE BATHROOM. ALL BEDROOMS NON-SMOKING.
PUNCH TAVERNS HOUSE WITH REAL ALE. CHILDREN WELCOME. BAR AND RESTAURANT MEALS.
NON-SMOKING AREAS. STOWMARKET 5 MILES. S££, D££.

Derbyshire

Dog & Partridge Country Inn

Mary and Martin Stelfox welcome you to a family-run 17th century Inn and Motel set in five acres, five miles from Alton Towers and close to Dovedale and Ashbourne. We specialise in family breaks, and special diets and vegetarians are catered for. All rooms have private bathrooms, colour TV, direct-dial telephone, tea-making facilities and baby listening service.

Ideal for touring Stoke Potteries, Derbyshire Dales and Staffordshire Moorlands. Open Christmas and New Year.

'Staffs Good Food Winners 2003/2004'.

Restaurant open all day, non-residents welcome

e-mail: info@dogandpartridge.co.uk
Tel: 01335 343183 • www.dogandpartridge.co.uk
Swinscoe, Ashbourne DE6 2HS

MOST BEDROOMS WITH PRIVATE BATHROOM. REAL ALE. CHILDREN AND PETS WELCOME. BAR MEALS. ASHBOURNE 3 MILES. S£££/££££, D££.

Rates

S – SINGLE ROOM rate   D – Sharing DOUBLE/TWIN ROOM

S£ D£ = Under £35   S££ D££ = £36-£45   S£££ D£££ = £46-£55   S££££ D££££ = Over £55

This is meant as an indication only and does not show prices for Special Breaks, Weekends, etc. Guests are therefore advised to verify all prices on enquiring or booking.

Derbyshire

THE MIDLANDS

Bentley Brook Inn is a busy country inn in the beautiful Peak Park, providing quality accommodation, an award-winning restaurant and an all-day bar offering informal meals and snacks. The Inn has a large child and pet-friendly garden. Favourite centre for walking and for visiting Dovedale, the Manifold Valley, Chatsworth and Alton Towers. Eleven refurbished en suite rooms of great character. Residents' lounge. Free wireless broadband in the bar. Pets welcome by prior arrangement.

Bentley Brook Inn

Fenny Bentley, Ashbourne, Derbyshire DE6 1LF
Tel: 01335 350278 • Fax: 01335 350422
e-mail: all@bentleybrookinn.co.uk
www.bentleybrookinn.co.uk

11 BEDROOMS, ALL WITH PRIVATE BATHROOM. ALL BEDROOMS NON-SMOKING.
CHILDREN AND PETS WELCOME. RESTAURANT MEALS.
ASHBOURNE 2 MILES. S££, D££££.

THE CROWN INN
MARSTON MONTGOMERY

Situated at the southern edge of the Peak District, The refurbished Crown Inn retains its original charm and character. All seven bedrooms have en suite facilities and a colour TV with teletext, a radio and tea & coffee making facilities. Creative menus based on the very best local produce offer daily specials. Carefully selected wine list features a good selection from around the world.

Riggs Lane, Marston Montgomery, Ashbourne, Derbyshire DE6 2FF
Tel: 01889 591 430 • e-mail: info@thecrowninnderbyshire.co.uk
www.thecrowninnderbyshire.co.uk

7 BEDROOMS, ALL WITH PRIVATE BATHROOM. ALL BEDROOMS NON-SMOKING. REAL ALE.
CHILDREN AND PETS WELCOME. BAR AND RESTAURANT MEALS.
ASHBOURNE 7 MILES. ££££.

THE YORKSHIRE BRIDGE INN (on facing page)

14 BEDROOMS, ALL WITH PRIVATE BATHROOM. FREE HOUSE WITH REAL ALE.
CHILDREN AND PETS WELCOME. BAR AND RESTAURANT MEALS. NON-SMOKING AREAS.
HATHERSAGE 2 MILES. S£££, D££.

The Yorkshire Bridge Inn

1826

- Glorious Peak District location
- Fantastic real ales
- Fine food prepared to order
- Fresh local produce
- 14 comfortable bedrooms
- Friendly atmosphere for all

Freehouse of the year
finalist 2000, 2001 & 2004

Call 01433 651361 for a brochure
web: www.yorkshire-bridge.co.uk

The Church Inn

Main Street, Chelmorton, Buxton SK17 9SL
Tel: 01298 85319 • www.thechurchinn.co.uk

Centrally located between Buxton and Bakewell, ideal for exploring the Peak District and North Derbyshire. A homely Inn with three double and one twin bedroom, all tastefully furnished and en suite. Colour TV and tea/coffee facilities. Wi-Fi access. The accommodation is in a separate annex from the pub. Off-street car parking.
Lunchtime and evening meals served from a varied menu. The bar has an excellent range of beers, wines and spirits.

4 BEDROOMS, ALL WITH PRIVATE BATHROOM. ALL BEDROOMS NON-SMOKING. FREE HOUSE WITH REAL ALE. BAR AND RESTAURANT MEALS.
BUXTON 4 MILES. S££. D££££.

For walking, climbing, mountain biking and caving visit Derbyshire. There are activities available at every level and courses to suit everyone. From the gently rolling farmland and National Forest in the south to the rugged demanding landscape of the Dark Peak in the north there are trails for cyclists and walkers to follow, many along old railway lines. Everyone can visit Poole's Cavern to see the best stalagmites and stalactites in Derbyshire (and discover the difference!), and the Blue John Cave at Castleton where this rare mineral is mined, and perhaps buy a sample of jewellery in one of the local shops. Buxton was a spa from Roman times, but the main attractions now are concerts, theatre and the annual literary and music festival. Concerts are held at Calke Abbey and at Chatsworth, the best known of the stately homes, with impressive interiors and magnificent gardens and grounds, and period dramas at Haddon Hall at Bakewell. Visit the market town of Chesterfield to see the church with the crooked spire, and for a step back in time go to Crich Tramway Village for a tram ride down a period street and on into the countryside.

Looking for holiday accommodation?
for details of hundreds of properties throughout the UK visit:
www.holidayguides.com

THE DEVONSHIRE ARMS (on facing page)

7 BEDROOMS, ALL WITH PRIVATE BATHROOM. ALL BEDROOMS NON-SMOKING. FREE HOUSE WITH REAL ALE. CHILDREN AND PETS WELCOME. BAR AND RESTAURANT MEALS. DESIGNATED COVERED SMOKING AREA.
CHAPEL-EN-LE-FRITH 4 MILES. S££. D££.

Derbyshire

Tel: 01298 23875 • www.devarms.com
e-mail: lesleywoodward@tiscali.co.uk

Set in the pictureque village of Peak Forest in the heart of the Peak District, the Devonshire Arms was once a coaching Inn, but today is a pub/hotel where our prime concern is your comfort, relaxation and enjoyment. The staff are here to ensure your visit exceeds your expectations and everyone can be certain of a warm welcome.

We have a large variety of rooms, all of which are en suite and individually styled and refurbished regularly. We are able to cater for couples, single people or families. Each bedroom has remote-control colour television, tea and coffee making facilities and hair dryer.

Dogs are welcome to stay and there is no extra charge. The Inn is privately owned, personally managed and has an enviable reputation for staff service, food and the accommodation we offer.

Prices from £32.50.

The Devonshire Arms

**Peak Forest,
Near Buxton,
Derbyshire
SK17 8EJ**

Situated in the picturesque village of Hathersage The Little John Inn offers a traditional pub atmosphere with local cask ales and home made food as well as accommodation right in the heart of the world famous Derbyshire Peak District.

After a fantastic day's walking in the surrounding peaks you can enjoy a selection of locally produced real ales including our own specially produced 'Little John' smooth bitter in our friendly traditional bar.

Our menu offers an excellent selection of home cooked meals with a daily specials board.

The Little John Inn has 6 en suite rooms and 3 self-catering cottages. All our accommodation comes with bedding and towels included in the price.

If you would like to make a booking or find out more please call
01433 650225

or e-mail: enquiries@littlejohnhotel.co.uk

THE LITTLE JOHN INN
Station Road, Hathersage
Hope Valley, Derbyshire S32 1DD

www.thelittlejohninn.co.uk

Owner Stephanie Bushell offers all guests a warm welcome.

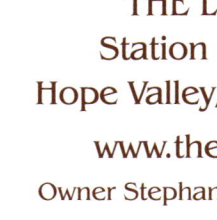

Herefordshire

The New Inn
Market Square, Pembridge, Leominster, Herefordshire HR6 9DZ
Tel: 01544 388427

The last battle of the Wars of the Roses was fought just a few miles from here at Mortimers Cross, and the treaty which gave England's crown to the Yorkist leader is believed to have been signed in the courtroom of this fourteenth century inn. Two ghosts are said to haunt the Inn: one a girl who appears only to women; the other a red-coated soldier armed with a sword.

A varied and interesting menu is offered at most reasonable prices in the bar, which has a log fire to warm it on chillier days, and the attractive lounge area is a popular venue for cosy evening dinners.

NO ACCOMMODATION. FREE HOUSE WITH REAL ALE. CHILDREN WELCOME.
BAR AND RESTAURANT MEALS. DESIGNATED COVERED SMOKING AREA.
KINGTON 6 MILES.

Please mention **Pubs & Inns of Britain** when making enquiries about accommodation featured in these pages

THE LITTLE JOHN HOTEL (on facing page)

6 BEDROOMS, ALL WITH PRIVATE BATHROOM. THREE COTTAGES. REAL ALE.
BAR MEALS. CHILDREN AND PETS WELCOME.
BAKEWELL 8 MILES.

Herefordshire — THE MIDLANDS

Saracens Head Inn
Symonds Yat East, Ross-on-Wye HR9 6JL

An ideal base from which to explore the Wye Valley and surrounding area.

Relax in the cosy lounge, stylish dining room or on the riverside terraces, with real ales or quality wines, and enjoy a wide variety of dishes using fresh ingredients, locally sourced wherever possible. Ten en suite bedrooms, eight overlooking the river, all with TV, tea/coffee making facilities and free Wi-Fi. This is a popular area with walkers, cyclists, canoeists and fishermen.
Sorry, no children (under 7 years) or pets.

AA INN ★★★★

Tel/Fax: 01600 890235 • contact@saracensheadinn.co.uk • www.saracensheadinn.co.uk

---

10 BEDROOMS, ALL WITH PRIVATE BATHROOM. ALL BEDROOMS NON-SMOKING. FREE HOUSE WITH REAL ALE.
BAR AND RESTAURANT MEALS.
MONMOUTH 4 MILES. S£££ABOVE. D££££.

The Royal Hotel
Palace Pound, Ross-on-Wye, Herefordshire HR9 5HZ
Tel: 01989 565 105 • Fax: 01989 768 058 • www.theroyal-ross.com

Charles Dickens and Queen Victoria are former visitors at the eye-catching Royal Hotel. Browse through the shops in the local market town or relax at the hotel with a cream tea and scone on the Riverside Terrace. Later, sample the extensive menu, perhaps with a real ale or fine wine. Accommodation is in 42 en suite rooms, each with a truly astonishing view.

Leicestershire & Rutland

The Mill on the Soar
Coventry Road, Broughton Astley, Leicestershire LE9 6QA
Tel: 01455 282419 • Fax: 01455 285937 • www.millonthesoar.co.uk

This friendly inn is ideal for a variety of purposes - romantic breaks, long weekends or business trips. Conferences are well catered for, with two delegate packages providing all modern facilities. A variety of room tariffs are offered – a family room accommodates two adults and one child. There is easy access to Birmingham, NEC and Rugby.

Fieldhead Hotel
Markfield Lane, Markfield , Leicester, Leicestershire LE67 9PS
Tel: 01530 245 454 • 01530 243 740 • www.fieldheadhotel-markfield.co.uk

The perfect meeting place for a reunion, wedding or birthday, with three function rooms, each capable of creating a unique atmosphere. The pub has an 'all day, every day' food policy and offers delicious seasonal menus. Accommodation is available in 28 en suite rooms, each with colour TV, wifi and coffee/tea making facilities.

The Wheatsheaf Inn
Brand Hill, Woodhouse Eaves, Leicestershire LE12 8SS
Tel: 01509 890320 • Fax: 01509 890891 • www.wheatsheafinn.net

Newly refurbished Inn, pub and restaurant offering the very best wines, real ales and beers, plus high quality cuisine, and luxurious accommodation in a cosy cottage annexe with twin and double rooms.

Rothley Court Hotel
Westfield Lane, Rothley, Leicestershire LE7 7LG
Tel: 0116 237 4141 • Fax: 0116 237 4483 • www.rothleycourthotel-leicester.co.uk

Rothley Court is deservedly popular for the vast array of luxuries and activities on offer, with its own trout-filled river as well as 'Karmaroma' Beauty & Holistic Therapy. Expect quality meals in the restaurant and a fine selection of ales and fine wines at the bar. Accommodation is in 30 en suite rooms, all with modern facilities.

Northamptonshire

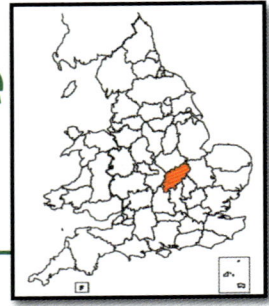

THE FALCON HOTEL
Castle Ashby, Northampton, Northamptonshire NN7 1LF
Tel: 01604 696 200 • Fax: 01604 696 673 • www.falconhotel-castleashby.com

With Silverstone and Stratford-upon-Avon only a short distance away, one can be assured of an outstanding level of modern English cuisine and excellent service at The Falcon. Accommodation can be found in the hotel itself or in one of the cottages next door. Each room is en suite with a full range of modern facilities.

The Swan at Lamport
Harborough Road, Lamport, Northamptonshire NN6 9EZ
Tel: 01604 686 555 • www.theswanatlamport.co.uk

The Swan at Lamport is the ideal place to come on sunny days and rainy afternoons! It features a stylish interior and offers a carefully selected stock of wines and real ales. All dishes on the varied menu are prepared from fresh ingredients.

The Talbot Hotel
New Street, Oundle, Northamptonshire PE8 4EA
Tel: 01832 273 621 • Fax: 01832 274 545 • www.thetalbot-oundle.com

Much of this fine building was built from the ruins of Fotheringhay Castle, which has associations with Mary, Queen of Scots, and it is rumoured that her spirit haunts the hotel. Accommodation is in 35 uniquely designed en suite bedrooms, each with modern facilities and modem plug-in points.

Saracens Head Hotel
219 Watling Street West, Towcester, Northants NN12 6BX
Tel: 01327 350 414 • Fax: 01327 359 879 • www.saracenshead-towcester.co.uk

This sturdy hotel dates back to the 19th century and is mentioned in Dickens' first novel, 'The Pickwick Papers'. Very popular in the town, it is renowned for wholesome meals such as fish and chips, and steaks cooked to your liking. Accommodation is in 21 en suite bedrooms. There is easy access to Towcester and Silverstone racecourses.

Nottinghamshire

The Chesterfield at Bingham
Church Street, Bingham, Nottinghamshire NG13 8AL
Tel: 01949 837342 • www.restaurantpubvaleofbelvoir.co.uk

A gastro pub retaining several original features, the Chesterfield offers an imaginative menu of dishes prepared from locally sourced ingredients, and diners may eat alfresco in the delightful beer garden. For a pint of your favourite draught beer or real ale, The Chesterfield is the ideal place.

THE CHESTERFIELD ARMS
Main Road, Gedling, Nottingham, Nottinghamshire NG4 3HL • Tel: 01159 878686

Located in the peaceful village of Gedling, with pretty hanging baskets outside, this eye-catching pub is devoted to sport, with live fixtures shown on screens throughout. Food is affordably priced and entertainment includes quiz and race nights.

The Travellers Rest
Mapperley Plains, Nottingham, Nottinghamshire NG3 5RT
Tel: 0115 9264412 • Fax: 0115 9203134

This superb pub is set in rural surroundings, yet with easy access to Nottingham town centre. Chef & Brewer pubs are known for serving mouthwatering dishes at affordable prices; the speciality here is a fresh fish supper. Why not sample one of the pub's quality wines or real ales to accompany your meal?

The Fiveways
Edwards Lane, Nottingham, Nottinghamshire NG5 3HU • Tel. 0115 9265612

Edwardian-style woodcarvings enhance the traditional exterior of this old coaching house, where refreshment is reasonably priced and the choice is extensive. Facilities include a piano room, a beer garden and two smoking shelters.

The Goose at Gamston

Gamston, Nottingham, Nottinghamshire NG2 6NA • Tel: 0115 9821041

The Goose is positioned in idyllic surroundings in Gamston and is an ideal family retreat, especially during summer months. The interior is elegant, with high ceilings and traditional wooden beams. The menu offers a wide range of tasty dishes, and for children (or big kids), there is ice cream!

THE THREE PONDS

Kimberley Road, Nuthall, Nottingham, Nottinghamshire NG16 1DA
Tel: 0115 9383170 • Fax: 0115 9382153

A friendly pub with an extensive menu of home-made dishes served in generous portions. The bar is stocked with a good selection of high quality real ales and draught beers. Regular activities include a popular quiz night and a poker night.

The Windsor Castle

Carlton Hill, Carlton, Nottingham, Nottinghamshire NG4 1EB • Tel: 0115 9871374

Since its refurbishment two years ago, this lively pub now boasts its very own stage and dance floor. Sport is important here, with live matches shown on the big screen, and customers can enjoy watching the game with a pint of their favourite ale and a tasty snack.

The Rose & Crown

Derby Road, Lenton, Nottingham, Nottinghamshire NG7 2GW • Tel: 0115 9784958

Situated in Lenton, Nottingham's student area, the Rose & Crown is a lively pub where good food is served and great company is free! Amenities include a beer garden, DJs, live music, a pool table, dart board, five TVs and a big screen for live sporting fixtures.

The Tree Tops

Plains Road, Mapperley, Nottingham, Nottinghamshire NG3 5RF
Tel: 0115 9558989 • Fax: 0115 9674031

Located just outside Nottingham in rural surroundings, and ideal for a peaceful lunchtime drink, the Tree Tops is cosy, with printed wallpaper and comfy sofas. The bar is stocked with real ales kept to a first class standard, and traditional pub food is available throughout the day.

The Ferry Inn

Main Road, Wilford, Nottingham, Nottinghamshire NG11 7AA
Tel: 0115 981 1441 • Fax: 0115 982 5089

Wilford is a quaint little village with a river flowing through it, and the pub is like something out of a fairytale, with low ceilings, real inglenook fires, wood-panelled recesses and attractive hanging baskets. Chef & Brewer pubs are renowned for serving superb food made from fresh ingredients, plus a good selection of quality beers, real ales and fine wines.

Shropshire

The Four Alls Inn & Motel

Newport Road,
Woodseaves,
Market Drayton
TF9 2AG

A warm welcome is assured at the Four Alls, situated in a quiet location of Woodseaves yet only a mile from the town of Market Drayton, and within easy reach of Shropshire's premier attractions.

Relax in our spacious bar, sample our home-cooked food and excellent traditional beers, then enjoy a good night's sleep in one of our nine en suite chalet-style rooms with central heating, TV and tea/coffee making facilities. The function room is available for weddings, celebrations or as a conference venue and can accommodate 50-100. Large car park.

Tel: 01630 652995 • Fax: 01630 653930
e-mail: inn@thefouralls.com • www.thefouralls.com

9 BEDROOMS, ALL WITH PRIVATE BATHROOM. ALL BEDROOMS NON-SMOKING. REAL ALE.
BAR AND RESTAURANT MEALS.
SHREWSBURY 18 MILES. S££, D£.

FREE or **REDUCED RATE** entry to Holiday Visits and Attractions – see our **READERS' OFFER VOUCHERS** on pages 179-204

Warwickshire

The Coleshill Hotel
152-156 High Street, Coleshill, Warwickshire B46 3BG
Tel: 01675 465 527 • Fax: 01675 464 013 • www.coleshillhotel.co.uk

The Coleshill is a popular haunt, with a heated outdoor terrace and delightfully named fireside 'Nook'. Birmingham NEC is just three miles away, and the city centre is convenient for a burst of retail therapy. Accommodation is spread over two buildings, with a Georgian annexe across the road. Each room is en suite, and rates include a full English breakfast.

THE MILLERS HOTEL
Twycross Road, Sibson, Nuneaton, Warwickshire CV13 6LB
Tel: 01827 880 223 • Fax: 01827 880 990 • www.millershotel-sibson.com

Sibson's former village bakery is now a superb conference and training centre and is perfect for weddings and birthday celebrations. Accommodation is en suite with all modern facilities. The Bar/Restaurant serves modern and traditional snacks and meals, real ale and carefully selected wines. Easy access to East Midlands Airport and Birmingham NEC.

Think of Warwickshire, and Shakespeare and Stratford-on-Avon immediately come to mind. A great way to see round this interesting town of black and white, half-timbered buildings is to take a guided walking tour, or better still, hire a bike. A cruise on the river offers a more gentle approach to sightseeing, perhaps after an exhausting morning exploring the wonderful range of shops, and for something different, visit the Butterfly Farm. Finally round off the day with a performance by the RSC at the newly rebuilt Royal Shakespeare Theatre next to the river. As well as Sir Basil Spence's Coventry Cathedral and two other churches designed by him, Coventry is home to Warwick Arts Centre, the largest in the Midlands, and there's an Art Trail to follow alongside Coventry Canal. The reconstructed Roman fort, the 16th century weaver's cottage and Coventry Transport Museum all illustrate different aspects of this city's development through the ages.

FHG Guides publish a large range of well-known accommodation guides. We will be happy to send you details or you can use the order form at the back of this book.

Worcestershire

The Anchor Inn
Main Road, Wyre Piddle, Pershore, Worcestershire WR10 2JB
Tel: 01386 556059 • www.anchorwyrepiddle.co.uk

Formerly boatmen's cottages, the Anchor Inn has gardens overlooking the beautiful South Worcestershire countryside and a terraced area by the waterside. Draught beers, real ales and wines are available, and the menu features dishes prepared from locally sourced ingredients.

Perdiswell House
Droitwich Road, Worcester, Worcestershire WR3 7JU • Tel: 01905 451311

Popular pub and diner situated on the outskirts of Worcester, with lots of delightful features and facilities to make your visit as relaxing and enjoyable as possible. A children's play area called Fuzzy Ed's Fun House will keep the kids entertained while mum and dad relax.

The Talbot
8-10 Barbourne Road, Worcester, Worcestershire WR1 1HT • Tel: 01905 723744

The Talbot is a candidate for the best pub in town, with a whole host of facilities and weekly entertainment including live music, a pool table, dart board and a beer garden – perfect for alfresco dining in summer months. Dishes on the menu are of a high standard and are prepared from the freshest ingredients.

THE MARWOOD
The Tything, Worcester, Worcestershire WR1 1JL
Tel: 01905 330 460 • www.themarwood.co.uk

Stunning Georgian establishment located in the tranquil Worcestershire countryside, with all traditional features including open log fires, a cosy restaurant and a lavish Champagne Terrace. This pub has character and stands out because of this, offering a good selection of beers, real ales and European lagers.

East Yorkshire

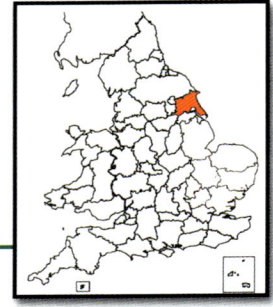

East Yorkshire is all about fun and action outdoors. From building sandcastles on the award-winning beaches along the North Sea coast in the east to walking in the Wolds inland, all the family will find an activity to enjoy. The Blue Flag beaches at Bridlington and Hornsea are ideal for children and if they tire of the sun and sand there's plenty of traditional entertainment too. Water sports aren't confined to the seaside, with windsurfing at Dacre Lakeside Park and jet skiing at Fossehill near Driffield, an ideal centre from which to explore both coast and country, and for golfers there's a choice of clifftop links and parkland courses inland and on the coast. For a taste of city life visit Hull, with its lovely waterfront, explore the Old Town while following the sculptures of the Seven Seas Fish Trail, enjoy modern drama at the Truck Theatre, and jazz, sea shanty and literature festivals, or watch football and rugby at the KC Stadium. Wherever you go, countryside, seaside or city, you're sure of an interesting and fun time.

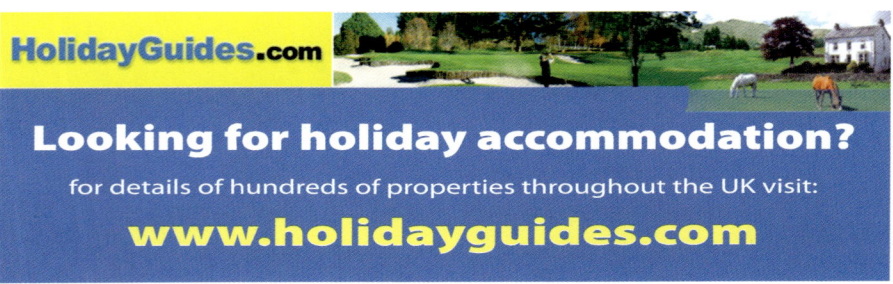

THE WOLDS INN (on facing page)

3 BEDROOMS, ALL WITH PRIVATE BATHROOM. ALL BEDROOMS NON-SMOKING. FREE HOUSE WITH REAL ALE. CHILDREN WELCOME. BAR MEALS, A LA CARTE MENU IN EVENINGS.
POCKLINGTON 6 MILES. S££, D£.

THE WOLDS INN
Driffield Road, Huggate, East Yorkshire YO42 1YH

A peaceful country inn in farming country high in the Wolds, the hostelry exudes an atmosphere well in keeping with its 16th century origins. Panelling, brassware and crackling fires all contribute to a mood of contentment, well supported in practical terms by splendid food, served either in the convivial bar, where home-made meals prepared from local produce are available daily at lunchtimes and in the evenings, or in the restaurant where choice may be made from a mouth-watering à la carte menu. Sunday roasts are also very popular.

Huggate lies on the Wolds Way and the inn is justly popular with walkers, whilst historic York and Beverley and their racecourses and the resorts of Bridlington, Hornsea and Scarborough are within easy reach.

First-rate overnight accommodation is available, all rooms having en suite facilities, central heating, Freeview television and tea and coffee tray.

Tel: 01377 288217
huggate@woldsinn.freeserve.co.uk
www.woldsinn.co.uk

AA ★★★ Inn

Accommodation Standards: Star Grading Scheme

The AA, VisitBritain, VisitScotland, and the VisitWales now use a single method of assessing and rating serviced accommodation. Irrespective of which organisation inspects an establishment the rating awarded will be the same, using a common set of standards, giving a clear guide of what to expect. They have full details of the grading system on their websites.

www.enjoyEngland.com     www.visitScotland.com

 www.visitWales.com   www.theaa.com

Using a scale of 1-5 stars the objective quality ratings give a clear indication of accommodation standard, cleanliness, ambience, hospitality, service and food.

This shows the full range of standards suitable for every budget and preference, and allows visitors to distinguish between the quality of accommodation and facilities on offer in different establishments.
All types of board and self-catering accommodation are covered, including hotels, B&Bs, holiday parks, campus accommodation, hostels, caravans and camping, and boats.

Gold and Silver awards are given to Hotels and Guest Accommodation that provide exceptional quality, especially in service and hospitality.

The more stars, the higher level of quality

★
acceptable quality; simple, practical, no frills

★★
good quality, well presented and well run

★★★
very good level of quality and comfort

★★★★
excellent standard throughout

★★★★★
exceptional quality, with a degree of luxury

National Accessible Scheme Logos for mobility impaired and older people

If you have particular mobility impairment. look out for the National Accessible Scheme. You can be confident of finding accommodation or attractions that meet your needs by looking for the following symbols.

 Older and less mobile guests
If you have sufficient mobility to climb a flight of steps but would benefit from fixtures and fittings to aid balance.

 Part-time wheelchair users
You have restricted walking ability or may need to use a wheelchair some of the time and can negotiate a maximum of 3 steps.

 Independent wheelchair users
You are a wheelchair user and travel independently. Similar to the international logo for independent wheelchair users.

 Assisted wheelchair users
You're a wheelchair user and travel with a friend or family member who helps you with everyday tasks.

North Yorkshire

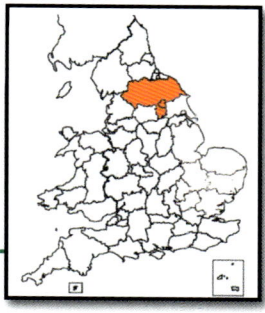

George & Dragon Inn
Aysgarth
Leyburn DL8 3AD
Tel: 01969 663358
Fax: 01969 663773

A warm welcome awaits you at this 17th century Coaching Inn. Set in the heart of the Yorkshire Dales National Park, near the spectacular Aysgarth Falls, this is an ideal base from which to explore this beautiful area.

There are seven en suite rooms, including a double room with a four-poster bed and a family room, each with flat screen TV, free wireless internet and tea/coffee facilities. Enjoy freshly prepared dishes using local ingredients; a private dining room is available by arrangement.

Sightseeing in the surrounding area includes the breathtaking waterfalls, moors and historic buildings.

info@georgeanddragonaysgarth.co.uk
www.georgeanddragonaysgarth.co.uk

7 BEDROOMS, ALL WITH PRIVATE BATHROOM. ALL BEDROOMS NON-SMOKING. FREE HOUSE WITH REAL ALE. CHILDREN AND PETS WELCOME. BAR AND RESTAURANT MEALS.
LEYBURN 7 MILES. S£££, D£££.

Visit the FHG website
www.holidayguides.com
for details of the wide choice of accommodation featured in the full range of FHG titles

Just a few minutes' drive from the A1, The Green Dragon in the attractive little village of Exelby dates back to the early 18th century and boasts an excellent restaurant, comfortable, well appointed accommodation and a large car park. The Green Dragon is a family-run, independent country inn taking pride in its friendly welcoming service. In winter the open log fires provide a warm, cosy atmosphere, whilst in the summer visitors can enjoy the decked area for alfresco eating.

Inside the recently refurbished inn you can choose to eat in the bar or in the spacious and attractive restaurant. Daily specials are also available every lunchtime and evening, and food is home cooked and locally sourced wherever possible. Food is served until 9pm (8pm Sundays).

To accompany your meal, there's a good selection of fine wines and excellent real ales, up to three of them on tap at any one time, with Black Sheep Best Bitter and Theakston's Black Bull as the regular brews, plus a guest ale. Live music and Theme Nights, plus Quiz Nights on Tuesdays.

There are four tastefully decorated and furnished rooms, (two doubles, one twin and one single), all en suite, with colour television and hospitality tray.

Exelby village is approximately two miles from the delightful market town of Bedale, the "Gateway to Wensleydale", which has a good range of shops, pubs, restaurants and a leisure centre.

The Green Dragon
High Row, Exelby, Bedale DL8 2HA
tel: 01677 422233
e-mail: jean@thegreendragonexelby.com
www.thegreendragonexelby.com

4 BEDROOMS, ALL EN SUITE. CHILDREN WELCOME. REAL ALE.
RESTAURANT MEALS.
BEDALE 2 MILES.

The Three Fiddles
34 Westgate, Guisborough, North Yorkshire TS14 6BA • Tel: 01287 63241

The Three Fiddles is situated in the busy market town of Guisborough. Food is prepared from fresh ingredients and served throughout the day, and amenities include a children's bouncy castle and a beer garden. Accommodation is in five rooms, all with colour TV and tea/coffee making facilities.

Rates
S – SINGLE ROOM rate   D – Sharing DOUBLE/TWIN ROOM

S£ D£ = Under £35   S££ D££ = £36-£45   S£££ D£££ = £46-£55   S££££ D££££ = Over £55

This is meant as an indication only and does not show prices for Special Breaks, Weekends, etc. Guests are therefore advised to verify all prices on enquiring or booking.

NEW INN (on facing page)

19 BEDROOMS, ALL WITH PRIVATE BATHROOM. ENTERPRISE INNS HOUSE WITH REAL ALE.
CHILDREN AND PETS WELCOME. BAR MEALS, RESTAURANT EVENINGS ONLY.
SETTLE 5 MILES. S£££, D£££.

New Inn

Clapham
'As relaxed as you like'

Quality Accommodation in the Yorkshire Dales.

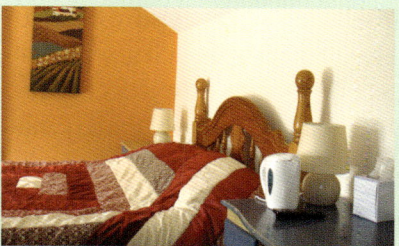

★★★ INN

Nestling beneath Ingleborough, the beautiful old village straddles either side of Clapham Beck, linked by three bridges. The church is at the top, the New Inn at the bottom.

This family-run inn is set amidst a geological wonderland of limestone, cavern and fell country.

Walk from our doorstep or tour the Dales or Lake District, Windermere being only a 40 minute drive away.

Experience the warmth and friendliness that we bring to the New Inn, a true 18th Century village coaching inn, now with 19 bedrooms, 2 bars with open fires, cask beers, quality wines and a range of single malt whiskies, restaurant and residents' lounge

Clapham is situated 5 miles north of Settle along the A65.

New Inn, Clapham, Near Ingleton, North Yorkshire LA2 8HH
Tel: 015242 51203 • Fax: 015242 51824
e-mail: info@newinn-clapham.co.uk
www.newinn-clapham.co.uk

The Fox & Hounds Inn

Former 16th century coaching inn, now a high quality residential Country Inn & Restaurant set amidst the beautiful North York Moors. Freshly prepared dishes, using finest local produce, are served every lunchtime and evening, with selected quality wines and a choice of cask ales. Excellent en suite acccommodation is available. Open all year. Winter Breaks available November to March.

For bookings please Tel: 01287 660218
Ainthorpe, Danby, Yorkshire YO21 2LD
e-mail: info@foxandhounds-ainthorpe.com
www.foxandhounds-ainthorpe.com

★★★★ INN

7 BEDROOMS, ALL WITH PRIVATE BATHROOM. ALL BEDROOMS NON-SMOKING. FREE HOUSE WITH REAL ALE. CHILDREN AND PETS WELCOME. BAR AND RESTAURANT MEALS.
WHITBY 12 MILES. S£££, D£££.

The Cross Keys
Middlesbrough Road, Upsall, Guisborough, North Yorkshire TS14 6RW
Tel: 01287 610035

The Cross Keys is the meeting point for the local branch of CAMRA, and offers all the traditional attractions of the classic English pub, such as low oak beams, wood-panelled recesses and a beer garden where guests have the option of dining alfresco. 20 bedrooms with all modern facilities provide comfortable accommodation.

The Claro Beagle
Ripon Road, Harrogate, North Yorkshire HG1 2JJ • Tel: 01423 569974

A modern-style community pub, with a contemporary bright, fresh look. There is a sports area with pool tables, a dart board and a plasma screen showing live sporting fixtures. Free wifi facility throughout.

ROYAL OAK HOTEL (on facing page)

5 BEDROOMS, ALL WITH PRIVATE BATHROOM. REAL ALE. CHILDREN WELCOME. BAR AND RESTAURANT MEALS.
THIRSK 23 MILES, MIDDLESBROUGH 9. S££, D££.

Royal Oak Hotel

Great Ayton North Yorkshire

The Best in Yorkshire Hospitality

The Monaghan family have run The Royal Oak Hotel since 1978. This 18th Century rural hostelry is at the heart of the village. Original features include the beamed ceilings and welcoming log fires, and add to the charm and character of this traditional inn.

The Best Ales in Yorkshire

The lively public bar is popular with visitors and locals alike.

Good ales on tap include Theakston's Old Peculiar, Theakston's bitter, along with keg ales, lager, cider and a good range of wines and spirits.

The extensive choice of menu at the Royal Oak is not one for the indecisive. Ditherers will find themselves at closing time still unable to choose from the excellent choice.

Food is also available in the tastefully decorated, comfortably rustic bars, and guest bedrooms provide well appointed overnight accommodation, all being en suite, with central heating, colour television and tea-making facilities.

**Royal Oak Hotel
High Green, Great Ayton,
North Yorkshire TS9 6BW**
Tel: 01642 722361 • Fax: 01642 724047
e-mail: info@royaloak-hotel.co.uk
www.royaloak-hotel.co.uk

Derek and Linda Monaghan

Tel: 01756 760262
Fax: 01756 761024

WHITE LION INN
Cray, Buckden, Near Skipton, North Yorkshire BD23 5JB

Nestling at the head of Wharfedale, the White Lion has been tastefully restored to offer 11 bedrooms (10 en suite, one shared bathroom), while retaining its original beams, open log fires and stone-flagged floors. Traditional English fare is served in the bar or cosy dining room and the Inn provides a good choice of beers and spirits.

The Inn is in the very heart of the Yorkshire Dales and makes an ideal base for touring and walking. There are also many sporting activities locally, including pony trekking, rock climbing, pot holing and golf.

e-mail: admin@whitelioncray.com • www.whitelioncray.com

11 BEDROOMS, 10 EN SUITE. REAL ALE.
PETS WELCOME. BAR MEALS. NON-SMOKING AREAS.
BUCKDEN 2 MILES.

We have three rooms located in the main pub building on the first floor and three more rooms in the annex building. All rooms are en suite and strictly non smoking. Dogs are not allowed. We have no family rooms and cannot accept children less than 14 years of age.

Nestling beneath the rising fells of Langstrothdale, the inn stands in a stunning location overlooking the River Wharfe.

This traditional Dales Inn with flagged floors, stone walls and mullioned windows is the last remaining family-owned freehouse in the parish of Buckden, Upper Wharfedale.

Comfortable accommodation, quality home-cooked food, well kept cask beers from Black Sheep and Copper Dragon Breweries, together with an excellent selection of wines and malts, are on offer in our unique inn.

The George is centrally located in the Yorkshire Dales National Park and is ideal for touring or walking.

GEORGE INN
Kirk Gill, Hubberholme, Near Skipton, North Yorkshire BD23 5JE
Tel: 01756 760223
www.thegeorge-inn.co.uk

6 BEDROOMS, ALL WITH PRIVATE BATHROOM. ALL BEDROOM NON SMOKING. REAL ALE.
BAR MEALS.
KETTLEWELL 6 MILES. S££££. D££.

FREE or **REDUCED RATE** entry to Holiday Visits and Attractions – see our **READERS' OFFER VOUCHERS** on pages 179-204

YORKSHIRE

North Yorkshire

Nine miles north of York in the village of Huby in the Vale of York, the Motel is an ideal base for a couple of nights away to visit York (15 minutes to the nearest long-stay car park), or a longer stay to visit the East Coast of Yorkshire, the Dales, the Yorkshire Moors, Herriot Country, Harrogate and Ripon.

The Motel is situated behind the New Inn (a separate business) which, contrary to its name, is a 500-year old hostelry, originally an old coaching inn, and full of character. All rooms are en suite (singles, doubles, twin and family rooms), and have colour television and tea-making facilities. Good home cooking is served, including vegetarian meals, and a full English breakfast is a speciality.

THE NEW INN MOTEL
Main Street, Huby,
York YO61 1HQ
Tel: 01347 810219

Pets are welcome (by arrangement)
Special breaks always available
Telephone for brochure

www.newinnmotel.co.uk
enquiries@newinnmotel.freeserve.co.uk

£40-£55 (single)
£65-£75 (double)
Special rates for Short Breaks and weekly rates

AA Highly Commended Guest Accommodation

8 BEDROOMS (NON-SMOKING), ALL WITH PRIVATE BATHROOM. FREE HOUSE WITH REAL ALE. CHILDREN WELCOME. RESTAURANT MEALS.
YORK 9 MILES. S££, D££.

THE TRAVELLER'S REST
Crimple Lane, Crimple, Harrogate, North Yorkshire HG3 1DF
Tel: 01423 883960

An old fashioned, traditional public house near Harrogate town centre, with low oak beams, a delightful stone-floored section and a charming conservatory leading to the garden area, where alfresco diners can enjoy views of sheep, ducks and swans. Real ales and draught beers are served chilled during summer months.

The Squinting Cat
Lund House Green, Pannal Ash, Harrogate, North Yorkshire HG3 1QF
Tel: 01423 565650

The Squinting Cat is a Two For One public house set in rural surroundings just south of the town centre. Families love to come here for mouth-watering dishes at affordable prices, and facilities include a children's 'Wacky Warehouse' play area and a large beer garden.

FHG Guides publish a large range of well-known accommodation guides. We will be happy to send you details or you can use the order form at the back of this book.

THE FORRESTERS ARMS HOTEL

Dating from the 12th century, this is one of England's oldest inns. The Henry Dee Bar still retains evidence of the days when it was the stable and the cosy lower bar has an unusual rounded stone chimney breast where log fires exude cheer in chilly weather.

Both bars are furnished with the work of Robert Thompson (the 'Mouseman') who carved a tiny mouse on every piece of furniture produced.

Real ale is available in convivial surroundings and ample and well-presented Yorkshire fare will more than satisfy the healthiest appetite.

This is the heart of James Herriot Country, within the North York Moors National Park, and the hotel is well recommended as a touring base, having outstanding accommodation.

Proud to be a pub that serves good food, not a restaurant that serves beer

The Forresters Arms, Kilburn, North Yorkshire YO61 4AH
Tel: 01347 868386 • e-mail: admin@forrestersarms.com • www.forrestersarms.com

9 BEDROOMS, ALL WITH PRIVATE BATHROOM. ALL BEDROOMS NON-SMOKING. REAL ALE.
CHILDREN AND PETS WELCOME. BAR AND RESTAURANT MEALS.
THIRSK 6 MILES. S£££, D££.

THE SOUTHERN CROSS
Dixons Bank, Middlesbrough, North Yorkshire TS7 8NX • Tel: 01642 317539

A large pub situated on a main road in the suburbs of Middlesbrough. Downstairs is a sports bar with four plasma screens, so there's no chance of missing that all important football match. The Two for One Menu is very popular amongst the locals at lunchtimes, and there are regular quizzes and live music.

The Three Jolly Sailors
Burniston, Scarborough, North Yorkshire YO13 0HJ • Tel: 01723 871628

Situated in the quaint village of Burniston just north of Scarborough is this Grade II Listed pub, an ideal stopoff point for ramblers on the Smugglers Walk between Scarborough and Whitby. All dishes are freshly prepared from locally sourced ingredients whenever possible.

A useful index of towns/counties appears on pages 205-206

The Scarborough
Market Lane, Eastfield, Scarborough, North Yorkshire YO11 3YN
Tel: 01723 582444 • Fax: 01723 582443

A Hungry Horse pub serving food and drink over four floors, with a children's play area on the top floor – a safe and secure place to keep youngsters entertained while parents relax. There is a beer garden, and regular events include pool competitions, karaoke and DJ/fun nights.

The Griffin
42 Micklegate, Selby, North Yorkshire YO8 0EQ
Tel: 01757 703227 • Fax: 01757 704574

A popular spot on the market square in Selby, recently refurbished to create an uplifting atmosphere, with contemporary lighter shades and stylish furnishings. Regular activities include three pool tables, a weekly quiz, karaoke and a live DJ at weekends.

The Londesborough Hotel
Market Place, Selby, North Yorkshire YO8 4NS
Tel: 01757 707355 • Fax: 01757 701607

Brimming with tradition, this friendly bar stocks a good selection of beers, ales and wines, and the kitchen brigade prepares quality meals to suit all tastes. Accommodation is in 23 Laura Ashley-style luxury bedrooms, almost all en suite.

The Windmill
16 - 20 Blossom Street, York, North Yorkshire YO24 1AJ • Tel: 01904 624834

This is a popular and contemporary venue situated in York centre. The menu offers an ample choice of delicious dishes and the bar is stocked with a wide range of drinks. Comfortable accommodation and good service make this an even more attractive prospect.

Lendal Cellars
26 Lendal, York, North Yorkshire YO1 8AA • Tel: 01904 623121

Traditional cellar bar situated in the picturesque city of York, with food available from an exciting menu including burgers and other pub food favourites. The bar is well stocked, with guest real ales, lagers, beers and wines. Features include an open-mic night, live bands and an outdoor pool table. Children welcome when dining.

HolidayGuides.com
visit our website for details of hundreds of properties throughout Britain

Northumberland

The Bay Horse Inn
West Woodburn, Hexham NE48 2RX
Tel: 01434 270218 • Fax: 01434 270274

A delightful 18thC coaching inn, nestling by a stone bridge over the River Rede. On the A68, 6 miles from Otterburn, 20 miles from Corbridge, 24 miles from Newcastle Airport; ideally placed for Hadrian's Wall, Kielder Water, Alnwick and the Scottish Borders.

- Excellent home-cooked cuisine
- Lounge bar

7 bedrooms, 5 en suite, all individually decorated in a delightful cottage style, with colour TV, tea and coffee making facilities, hairdryer, ironing facilities and a trouser press.

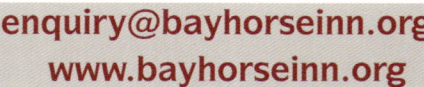

enquiry@bayhorseinn.org
www.bayhorseinn.org

7 BEDROOMS, 5 WITH PRIVATE BATHROOM. CHILDREN WELCOME.
BAR AND RESTAURANT MEALS.
OTTERBURN 6 MILES, CORBRIDGE 20 MILES.

THE ROB ROY (on facing page)

5 BEDROOMS, ALL WITH PRIVATE BATHROOM. ALL BEDROOMS NON-SMOKING.
CHILDREN WELCOME. BAR AND RESTAURANT MEALS.
BERWICK-UPON-TWEED 1 MILE. S££, D££££.

Dock Road, Tweedmouth Berwick-upon-Tweed Northumberland TD15 2BE

Your hosts Ian and Linda Woods extend to you the warmest welcome to this family-run Northumberland B&B.

Situated in Tweedmouth, in historic Berwick-upon-Tweed, the Rob Roy is a guest house in the classic, welcoming Northumberland style.

Perfect for Northumberland holidays and visitors keen to explore the open country, historic sites and remarkable coastline of this beautiful county.

Within easy walking distance of Berwick-upon-Tweed town centre and also Spittal beach and promenade.

The five bedrooms, three double rooms, one twin room, and a family room, all have en suite facilities and are comfortable and stylishly furnished with television, tea and coffee making facilities, alarm clocks and hairdryers. Free Wi-Fi is also available.

The guest lounge with real fire and stone walls is the perfect place to relax and can also be used for a private function or business meeting.

The fully licensed bar is well stocked with real ales and a selection of wines, while the popular beer garden is a great way to enjoy a drink whilst taking in the views of the River Tweed as it joins the North Sea.

Prices start from £60 per night for a double or twin room, £75 for the family room and £45 for single occupancy.

Prices include breakfast, chosen from a full English selection or alternatives. Lunches and dinners are also available at the Rob Roy in our Harbour Lights Restaurant, serving the best of fresh produce locally sourced wherever possible.

Tel & Fax: 01289 306428 • e-mail: therobroy@hotmail.co.uk

108 Northumberland   NORTH EAST ENGLAND

The Anglers Arms
A Legend in the very Heart of Northumberland

This traditional Coaching Inn is situated only 6 miles from Morpeth, beside picturesque Weldon Bridge on the River Coquet. Bedrooms are cosy and welcoming, with a touch of olde worlde charm. Be prepared for a hearty Northumbrian breakfast!

Meals can be be enjoyed in the friendly bar, or outdoors on sunny summer days; alternatively dine in style and sophistication in the à la carte Pullman Railway Carriage restaurant. Ideal for exploring both coast and country, the Inn also caters for fishermen, with its own one-mile stretch of the River Coquet available free to residents.

The Anglers Arms
Weldon Bridge, Longframlington,
Northumberland NE65 8AX
Tel: 01665 570271/570655
Fax: 01665 570041
info@anglersarms.fsnet.co.uk
www.anglersarms.com

8 BEDROOMS, ALL WITH PRIVATE BATHROOM. FREE HOUSE WITH REAL ALE.
CHILDREN WELCOME. BAR AND RESTAURANT MEALS. NON-SMOKING AREAS.
ROTHBURY 5 MILES. S£££, D££££.

Please mention **Pubs & Inns** of **Britain**
when making enquiries about accommodation featured in these pages

---

Rates S – SINGLE ROOM rate   D – Sharing DOUBLE/TWIN ROOM

S£ D£ = Under £35   S££ D££ = £36-£45   S£££ D£££ = £46-£55   S££££ D££££ = Over £55

This is meant as an indication only and does not show prices for Special Breaks, Weekends, etc.
Guests are therefore advised to verify all prices on enquiring or booking.

BATTLESTEADS COUNTRY HOTEL & RESTAURANT (on facing page)

17 BEDROOMS, ALL WITH PRIVATE BATHROOM. ALL BEDROOMS NON-SMOKING.
PETS WELCOME. BAR MEALS.
NEWCASTLE 20 MILES. S££££, D£££.

Battlesteads Country Hotel & Restaurant

Hexham
Northumberland

Originally built as a farmstead in 1747, this Hotel and Restaurant features a well stocked bar and cosy fireplace with wood-burning stove in the winter, and a sunny conservatory within a secret walled garden for enjoying the sunshine.

Battlesteads features excellent bar meals and à la carte menus. Our bar has 5 cask-ales including Durham Magus, Wylam Gold Tankard and both Black Sheep Ale and Black Sheep Special, and our wine list runs to over 20 varieties.

This friendly, family-run hotel, with 17 en suite bedrooms, including ground floor rooms with disabled access, is ideally placed for Hadrian's Wall, Kielder and Border Reiver Country. Pets welcome by arrangement.

Battlesteads Hotel, Wark on Tyne, Hexham, Northumberland NE48 3LS
Tel: (01434) 230 209 • Fax: (01434) 230 039
e-mail: info@battlesteads.com
www.battlesteads.com

COOK AND BARKER INN

Two families with historic associations with the village of Newton-on-the-Moor have given their names to this sturdily-built stone inn which lies just off the A1, offering a peaceful haven for business travellers and holidaymakers alike. With an excellent reputation locally – and indeed, farther afield (good news travels!), the creative kitchen brigade use only the best and freshest of ingredients to produce tempting à la carte menus; bar lunches are also available, and in finer weather can be enjoyed in the attractive beer garden.

Accommodation is of an equally high standard, all the cosy bedrooms having en suite facilities, colour television, tea/coffee maker and DVD player as standard. Add to these virtues a friendly welcome and efficient service, and you have all the ingredients for a relaxing break.

Newton-on-the-Moor, Felton, Morpeth, Northumberland NE65 9JY
Tel & Fax: 01665 575234 • www.cookandbarkerinn.co.uk

18 BEDROOMS, ALL WITH PRIVATE BATHROOM. ALL BEDROOMS NON-SMOKING. FREE HOUSE WITH REAL ALE. CHILDREN WELCOME. BAR AND RESTAURANT MEALS.
ALNWICK 5 MILES. S£££££, D£££££.

Rambling over the heather-clad Cheviot moorlands, exploring the castles and pele towers built to ward off invading Scots, watching the feast of wildlife on the coast and in the countryside, breathing in the wonderful sea air on a golden sandy beach, you'll find it all in Northumberland. On the coast, a designated Area of Outstanding Natural Beauty, keen walkers can take the Coast Path from the walled Georgian market town of Berwick-on-Tweed to Cresswell, stopping at little fishing villages on the way. For a shorter route, follow the section along Embleton beach from Craster, best known for its traditionally smoked kippers, to get the best views of the ruins of Dunstanburgh Castle. At the lively market town of Alnwick visit the castle, Hogwarts in the Harry Potter films, with the newly redeveloped gardens, magnificent water features and even a poison garden! Rare and endangered wildlife is found all along the coast and the ultimate destination for enthusiasts is the Farne Islands, with boat trips from the family resort of Seahouses to watch the grey seals and seabirds, including puffins, in the breeding seasons. Wildlife is abundant in the uplands to the west too. In the heather moorlands of the Cheviot Hills there are plenty of opportunities for birdwatching, as well as horse riding, fishing, canoeing and rock climbing. Learn too about the Romans by watching a re-enactment of Roman life at one of the settlements along Hadrian's Wall, or walk along its length from coast to coast. Hexham and Haltwhistle are good bases for a visit, and these and other market towns and villages make a stay here a very pleasant one.

THE OLDE SHIP INN

Main Street,
Seahouses,
Northumberland
NE68 7RD
Tel: 01665 720200
Fax: 01665 720383

A former farmhouse dating from 1745, the inn stands overlooking the harbour in the village of Seahouses.

The Olde Ship, first licensed in 1812, has been in the same family for 100 years and is now a fully residential hotel. All guest rooms, including three with four-poster beds, and executive suites with lounges and sea views, are en suite, with television, refreshment facilities and direct-dial telephone. The bars and corridors bulge at the seams with nautical memorabilia. Good home cooking features locally caught seafood, along with soups, puddings and casseroles

www.seahouses.co.uk • e-mail: theoldeship@seahouses.co.uk

18 BEDROOMS, ALL WITH PRIVATE BATHROOM. ALL BEDROOMS NON-SMOKING. FREE HOUSE WITH REAL ALE.
CHILDREN OVER 10 YEARS WELCOME IF STAYING IN HOTEL. BAR AND RESTAURANT MEALS.
BAMBURGH 3 MILES. S££££, D£££.

Other British holiday guides from FHG Guides

300 GREAT HOTELS
SHORT BREAK HOLIDAYS
The bestselling and original PETS WELCOME!
THE GOLF GUIDE – *Where to Play, Where to Stay*
500 GREAT PLACES TO STAY
SELF-CATERING HOLIDAYS • BED & BREAKFAST STOPS
CARAVAN & CAMPING HOLIDAYS • FAMILY BREAKS

Published annually: available in all good bookshops or direct from the publisher:
FHG Guides, Abbey Mill Business Centre, Seedhill, Paisley PA1 1TJ
Tel: 0141 887 0428 • Fax: 0141 889 7204
e-mail: admin@fhguides.co.uk • www.holidayguides.com

Tyne & Wear

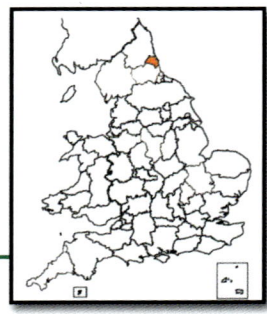

The Gold Medal
Chowdene Bank, Gateshead, Tyne and Wear NE9 6JP • Tel: 0191 4821549

Family pub situated in Gateshead, where drinks and food are served with a smile and both are reasonably priced and generous in quantity. There is regular entertainment, perhaps a quiz, live music, or even live sporting fixtures shown on the big screen.

The Guide Post
Makepeace Terrace, Springwell, Gateshead, Tyne & Wear NE9 7RR
Tel: 0191 4160298 • Fax: 0191 4179841

Situated between Gateshead and Washington, this popular spot attracts a friendly crowd made up of students, regulars and passers by. The food menu is popular, particularly the Sunday Roasts. Attractions include a pool table, dart board, and a big screen TV, plus regular quizzes and live music.

The Beaconsfield
Beaconsfield Road, Low Fell, Gateshead, Tyne and Wear NE9 5EU • Tel: 0191 4820125

Shades of cream, red ochre and sage green, plus suede seats and oak flooring, enhance the elegant decor of this modern venue in Gateshead. Hot and cold snacks are served throughout the day, every day, and live sporting fixtures are shown on large plasma screens.

Looking for holiday accommodation?
for details of hundreds of properties throughout the UK visit:
www.holidayguides.com

THE LONSDALE
West Jesmond, Newcastle-upon-Tyne, Tyne & Wear NE2 3HQ • Tel: 0191 2810039
Students love this pub venue situated in a popular area just outside West Jesmond. Customers enjoy the live sporting fixtures shown on the big screens, plasma screen or one of the other TVs. Attractions include two pool tables, quiz nights and live bands.

The Corner House
Heaton, Newcastle-upon-Tyne, Tyne & Wear NE6 5RP • Tel: 0191 2659602
Open-plan corner pub with a distinctive long bar, ideal for an after-work drink or meal. The staff are welcoming and add to the relaxed atmosphere. Facilities include a pool table, dart board, quizzes and big screen TVs. Accommodation is in 10 bedrooms (double, twin and family), all with modern facilities.

The Newton Park
**Longbenton, Newcastle-upon-Tyne, Tyne & Wear NE7 7EB
Tel: 0191 266 2010**
Situated next to the Ministry in Benton Park, this U-shaped open-plan bar boasts comfortable sofas and an imaginative food menu. Attractions include a games room, real ale bar, function room and dining area.

The Eye on The Tyne
Broad Chare, Newcastle-upon-Tyne, Tyne & Wear NE1 3DQ • Tel: 0191 2617385
Located in the middle of a prestigious part of the city centre, close to local hotels, and with the Law Courts nearby, this pub attracts a varied clientele. The in-house coffee shop serves coffee and freshly prepared food from 11am.

The Crows Nest
Percy Street, Newcastle-upon-Tyne, Tyne & Wear NE1 7RY • Tel: 0191 2612607
Formerly Bar Oz, the theme is fun, with fantastic food! Convenient for the two universities of Newcastle and Northumbria, the pub is very popular with students. It offers a good choice of draught beers and real ales, with a lively atmosphere during big matches shown on TV.

The Bourgognes
78 Newgate Street, Newcastle upon Tyne, Tyne & Wear NE1 5RQ • Tel: 0191 2326212
Located next to Eldon Square shopping centre and just a short distance from St James' football ground. With leather couches, wooden floors and carpeted recesses, this friendly pub is popular with students who appreciate the reasonably priced fare.

Cheshire

Tucked in a peaceful corner of rural Cheshire, the 300-year-old Pheasant Inn at Higher Burwardsley stands atop the Peckforton Hills, with the most magnificent panoramic views of the Cheshire plains. Whether you come to drink, dine or unwind for a few days in one of our 12 en suite bedrooms, this atmospheric location will quickly have you under its spell. Freshly cooked wholesome food using local produce is on the menu, rewarded for its quality with a listing in the Michelin Good Pub Guide and Egon Ronay Guide. Delightful old sandstone buildings, open log fires, and the friendly, cosy atmosphere all add to the magic!

The Pheasant Inn
Higher Burwardsley, Tattenhall
Cheshire CH3 9PF
Tel: 01829 770434 • Fax: 01829 771097
e-mail: info@thepheasantinn.co.uk • www.thepheasantinn.co.uk

12 BEDROOMS, ALL WITH PRIVATE BATHROOM. ALL BEDROOMS NON-SMOKING. FREE HOUSE WITH REAL ALE. CHILDREN AND PETS WELCOME. BAR AND RESTAURANT MEALS. CHESTER 9 MILES. S£££, D££.

THE PLOUGH AT EATON (on facing page)

17 BEDROOMS, ALL WITH PRIVATE BATHROOM. ALL BEDROOMS NON-SMOKING. FREE HOUSE WITH REAL ALE. CHILDREN WELCOME. BAR AND RESTAURANT MEALS. CONGLETON 2 MILES. S££££, D££££.

The Plough
AT EATON

**Macclesfield Road, Eaton,
Near Congleton, Cheshire CW12 2NH
Tel: 01260 280207 • Fax: 01260 298458**

Traditional oak beams and blazing log fires in winter reflect the warm and friendly atmosphere of this half-timbered former coaching inn which dates from the 17th century.

The heart of the 'Plough' is the kitchen where food skilfully prepared is calculated to satisfy the most discerning palate. Luncheons and dinners are served seven days a week with traditional roasts on Sundays.

In peaceful, rolling countryside near the Cheshire/Staffordshire border, this is a tranquil place in which to stay and the hostelry has elegantly colour-co-ordinated guest rooms, all with spacious bathrooms, LCD colour television, direct-dial telephone and tea and coffee-making facilities amongst their impressive appointments. Wireless internet access available.

**e-mail: theploughinn@hotmail.co.uk
www.theploughinnateaton.co.uk**

The De Trafford
Congleton Road, Alderley Edge, Cheshire SK9 7AA
Tel: 01625 583881 • Fax: 01625 586625

Cobblestone surroundings lead prospective visitors to this elegant inn located in Alderley Edge. Tradition is paramount, with open fires, candlelit tables and cosy nooks for private dining. Accommodation is next door – all bedrooms are en suite, with colour TV and tea/coffee making facilities.

The Shrewsbury Arms
Warrington Road, Mickle Trafford, Chester, Cheshire CH2 4EB • Tel: 01244 300309

The Shrewsbury Arms has everything one could want in a country pub – low oak beams, slate flooring and an impressive stock of cask ales, fine wines and beers. The pub's menu features traditional favourites prepared from fresh fish and locally sourced meat, and a Sunday Roast.

The Oaklands
93 Hoole Road, Chester, Cheshire CH2 3NB • Tel: 01244 345528

A peaceful spot set in an idyllic part of Chester, serving real ales, fine wines and hearty pub meals. There is regular entertainment, and large TV screens mean you can count on the Oaklands for those all-important football matches!

Bromfield Arms
43 Faulkener Street, Chester, Cheshire CH2 3BD • Tel: 01244 345037

Located close to the zoo in Chester is this Cask Marque accredited pub with a pool room and snug. Customers need no encouragement to sample the real ales and delicious meals on offer. There is a weekly quiz, and live sporting fixtures are shown on a large screen TV.

THE WHITE LION
Manley Road, Alvanley, Frodsham, Cheshire WA6 9DD • Tel: 01928 722949

Alvanley is an idyllic location with breathtaking views all around. The White Lion upholds all the traditional pub values, with wooden beams, good food and the warmth of two real fires in winter. There is a good choice of quality wines, real ales and draught beers.

Bestselling holiday accommodation guides for over 50 years

Cumbria

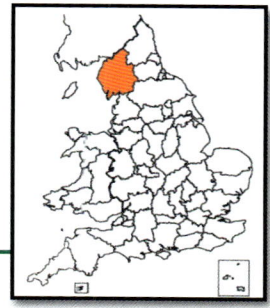

The Blacksmith's Arms offers all the hospitality and comforts of a traditional country inn. Enjoy tasty meals served in the bar lounges, or linger over dinner in the well-appointed restaurant. The inn is personally managed by the proprietors, Anne and Donald Jackson, who guarantee the hospitality one would expect from a family concern. Guests are assured of a pleasant and comfortable stay. There are eight lovely bedrooms, all en suite. Peacefully situated in the beautiful village of Talkin, the inn is convenient for the Borders, Hadrian's Wall and the Lake District. There is a good golf course, walking and other country pursuits nearby.

**Talkin Village, Brampton, Cumbria
CA8 1LE
Tel: 016977 3452
Fax: 016977 3396**

e-mail: blacksmithsarmstalkin@yahoo.co.uk • www.blacksmithstalkin.co.uk

8 BEDROOMS, ALL WITH PRIVATE BATHROOM. ALL BEDROOMS NON-SMOKING. FREE HOUSE WITH REAL ALE. BAR AND RESTAURANT MEALS.
CARLISLE 9 MILES. S££, D£.

Rates

S – SINGLE ROOM rate   D – Sharing DOUBLE/TWIN ROOM

S£ D£ = Under £35   S££ D££ = £36-£45   S£££ D£££ = £46-£55   S££££ D££££ = Over £55

This is meant as an indication only and does not show prices for Special Breaks, Weekends, etc. Guests are therefore advised to verify all prices on enquiring or booking.

Cumberland Inn

Tel: 01434 381875
Townfoot, Alston, Cumbria CA9 3HX
stay@cumberlandinnalston.com
www.cumberlandinnalston.com

A comfy retreat in the secluded North Pennines. Within reach of the Lake District National Park. Real beer, real fires and real hospitality await your arrival. Home-made hearty fare available all day to revive flagging spirits. Our 5 recently refurbished rooms are all en suite. An ideal base for walking, cycling and golfing.

★★★ INN

5 BEDROOMS, ALL WITH PRIVATE BATHROOM. ALL BEDROOMS NON-SMOKING. FREE HOUSE WITH REAL ALE. CHILDREN WELCOME. BAR AND RESTAURANT MEALS.
PENRITH 16 MILES. S££, D££.

The Black Cock Inn

Princes Street,
Broughton-in-Furness
Cumbria LA20 6HQ
Tel: 01229 716529
www.blackcockinncumbria.com

The Black Cock Inn stands at the heart of the attractive little town of Broughton-in-Furness, within easy reach of some of the Lake District's finest scenery. This much-loved village inn is full of history, charm and atmosphere. This 16th century Inn with its low beamed ceiling boasts a suntrap courtyard garden during the summer and a roaring log fire during the winter months, giving it a wonderful traditional ambience.

There's always a selection of real ales and lagers on offer in the bar which is open from morning 'til night, every day.

The inn has five comfortable and very well appointed en suite guest bedrooms.

There is excellent walking country in the area, with plenty of history and natural features to discover, and Broughton itself is well worth taking time to explore.

5 BEDROOMS, ALL WITH PRIVATE BATHROOM. FREE HOUSE WITH REAL ALES. CHILDREN AND PETS WELCOME. BAR AND RESTAURANT MEALS.
ULVERSTON 8 MILES. S££, D££.

THE SUN (on facing page)

8 BEDROOMS, ALL WITH PRIVATE BATHROOM. ALL BEDROOMS NON-SMOKING. FREE HOUSE WITH REAL ALE. CHILDREN AND PETS WELCOME. DINER. NON-SMOKING AREAS.
AMBLESIDE 6 MILES. S££, D££.

The Sun
CONISTON
★★★★

bar, diner & 4 star inn

The Sun in Coniston has been here for something like 400 years at the start of the mountains and the pack horse trails to the West. Forever associated with Donald Campbell and his world water speed record attempts, the pub remains a classic Lakeland Inn of rare quality.

It offers a unique mix of bar, diner & four star inn, with the kind of comfortable informality and atmosphere that many attempt but few achieve.

At its heart is a great bar with 8 real ales on hand-pull, 4 draft lagers, 20+ malts and 30+ wines. The food is freshly prepared using locally sourced ingredients and can be enjoyed in the bar, in the conservatory, outside on the front & on the terrace. The 8 recently refurbished ensuite bedrooms overlook the village with superb panoramic views. Extra thick mattresses & quality comforters help ensure a good nights sleep.

THE SUN CONISTON LA21 8HQ
tel 015394 41248   fax 015394 41219   email info@thesunconiston.com
www.thesunconiston.com

The Sun Inn

www.dentbrewery.co.uk

Main Street, Dent, Sedbergh, Cumbria LA10 5QL
Tel: 01539 625208 • e-mail: thesun@dentbrewery.co.uk

Dent, with its quaint narrow cobbled street lined with stone cottages, some dating from the 15th and 16th centuries, is within the Yorkshire Dales National Park and, completely unspoiled, is a most relaxing holiday venue. So, too, is the Sun's bar, a convivial retreat that will soon cast its spell on all who enter, a happy mood influenced not only by its coin-studded beams, open coal fire and fascinating collection of local photographs, but also by its traditional ales and tempting variety of straightforward meals.

A homely place in which to stay, this friendly hostelry has comfortable rooms with washbasin, colour television and tea and coffee-making facilities.

4 BEDROOMS. DENT BREWERY HOUSE WITH REAL ALE.
CHILDREN AND PETS WELCOME. BAR MEALS. NON-SMOKING AREAS.
SEDBERGH 4 MILES. S£, D£.

Book with this advert and claim a FREE bottle of French house wine at dinner

Elterwater, Langdale, Cumbria LA22 9HP
Tel: 015394 37210 • www.britinn.co.uk

A 500 year-old quintessential Lakeland Inn nestled in the centre of the picturesque village of Elterwater amidst the imposing fells of the Langdale Valley. Comfortable, quality en suite double and twin-bedded rooms. Dogs welcome. Enquire about our Mid-Week Special Offers. Relax in the oak-beamed Bars or Dining Room whilst sampling local real ales and dishes from our extensive menu of fresh, home-cooked food using lots of Cumbrian produce.
Quiz Night most Sundays.
e-mail: info@britinn.co.uk

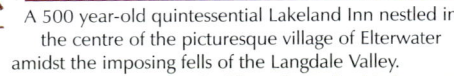

9 BEDROOMS, ALL WITH PRIVATE BATHROOM. ALL BEDROOMS NON-SMOKING. FREE HOUSE WITH REAL ALE.
CHILDREN AND PETS WELCOME. BAR MEALS, RESTAURANT EVENINGS ONLY.
AMBLESIDE 3 MILES. S££££, D£££.

THE BOOT INN (on facing page)

9 BEDROOMS, ALL WITH PRIVATE BATHROOM. REAL ALE. ALL BEDROOMS NON-SMOKING.
CHILDREN AND PETS WELCOME. BAR AND RESTAURANT MEALS.
RAVENGLASS 6 MILES. S££, D££.

The Boot Inn

Caroline & Sean welcome you to Boot Inn, dating in parts from 1570, and situated in the centre of the tiny village of Boot in Eskdale. This stunning valley offers superb walks for all abilities from a riverside stroll to an assault on Scafell straight from our door.

There are 9 comfortable en suite rooms, a lovely beer garden with separate children's play areas and wonderful fell views.

Pet-friendly.

In the restaurant, the bar or the conservatory, we offer a comprehensive menu and a daily Chef's Specials board. All our food is homemade using local produce wherever possible as we are very aware of the impact of 'food miles', including free range eggs from local farms, Bewley's beef and Cumberland Sausages, and local cheeses. We specialise in traditional hearty home cooking and baking.

Special Breaks regularly available on our website.

The Boot Inn, Boot, Eskdale, Cumbria CA19 1TG
Tel: 019467 23224
e-mail: enquiries@bootinn.co.uk
www.bootinn.co.uk

THE KINGS ARMS HOTEL
Hawkshead, Ambleside,
Cumbria LA22 0NZ
Tel: 015394 36372
www.kingsarmshawkshead.co.uk

Join us for a relaxing stay amidst the green hills and dales of Lakeland, and we will be delighted to offer you good food, homely comfort and warm hospitality in historic surroundings.

We hope to see you soon!

- SELF-CATERING COTTAGES ALSO AVAILABLE -

9 BEDROOMS, ALL WITH PRIVATE BATHROOM. ALL BEDROOMS NON-SMOKING. FREE HOUSE WITH REAL ALE. CHILDREN AND PETS WELCOME. BAR AND RESTAURANT MEALS. DESIGNATED COVERED SMOKING AREA. AMBLESIDE 4 MILES. S£££, D££.

Coledale INN
Braithwaite,
Near Keswick CA12 5TN
Tel: 017687 78272
Fax: 017687 78416

A friendly, family-run Victorian Inn in a peaceful hillside position above Braithwaite, and ideally situated for touring and walking, with paths to the mountains immediately outside our gardens. All bedrooms are warm and spacious, with en suite shower room and colour television. Children are welcome, as are pets. Home-cooked meals are served every lunchtime and evening, with a fine selection of inexpensive wines, beers and Jennings, Yates and Theakstons real cask ale. Open all year except midweek lunches in winter. Tariff and menu sent on request.

www.coledale-inn.co.uk
info@coledale-inn.co.uk

20 BEDROOMS, ALL WITH PRIVATE BATHROOM. FREE HOUSE WITH REAL ALE. CHILDREN AND PETS WELCOME. BAR AND RESTAURANT MEALS. NON-SMOKING AREAS. KESWICK 2 MILES. S£, D£.

HORSE & FARRIER INN (on facing page)

9 BEDROOMS, ALL WITH PRIVATE BATHROOM. FREE HOUSE WITH REAL ALE. CHILDREN WELCOME. BAR AND RESTAURANT MEALS. KESWICK 4 MILES.

Horse & Farrier Inn

Threkeld • Keswick • Cumbria

The Horse & Farrier has enjoyed an idyllic location in the centre of the picturesque village of Threlkeld, just 4 miles east of Keswick in Cumbria, for over 300 years. Built in 1688 and situated beneath Blencathra, with stunning views looking over towards the Helvellyn Range, this traditional Lakeland Inn offers a warm Cumbrian welcome to all its customers.

Mellow Lakeland stone, traditional architecture and such a peaceful setting make the Horse & Farrier a perfect place to enjoy a quiet pint, delicious food or a short break "away from it all". With superb Lakeland walks on your doorstep including Blencathra and Skiddaw and the Cumbria Way, we're ideally situated for walkers.

Our Restaurant is well known locally for the quality and imagination of its food and our Bar serves some of the best Jennings real ales in the Lake District.

Together with our well appointed en suite bed & breakfast accommodation, this really is a special place to spend some time.

Horse & Farrier Inn, Threlkeld, Keswick, Cumbria CA12 4SQ
Tel: 017687 79688 • Fax: 017687 79823
info@horseandfarrier.com • www.horseandfarrier.com

The Punch Bowl
Crosthwaite, Near Kendal, Cumbria LA8 8HR
Tel: 01539 568237 • Fax: 01539 568875 • www.the-punchbowl.co.uk

Low ceilings and oak beams are an attractive feature here, and log fires are cosy during the colder winter months. The patio overlooks the scenic Lyth Valley, and the comfortable accommodation has all modern facilities.

The Mortal Man Inn
Troutbeck, Windermere, Cumbria LA23 1PL
Tel: 01539 433193 • Fax: 01539 431261 • www.themortalman.co.uk

Poets, authors and painters alike have found inspiration from this delightful spot in the Troutbeck Valley. The alehouse turned inn offers quality real ales, carefully selected wines, and cosy bedrooms with modern facilities, and the cuisine is prepared from fresh, locally sourced ingredients whenever possible.

The Brackenrigg Inn
Watermillock, Ullswater, Penrith, Cumbria CA11 0LP
Tel: 01768 486206 • Fax: 01768 486945 • www.brackenrigginn.co.uk

The views of Ullswater and the Lakeland fells are a major attraction at this beautiful 18th century inn, which offers a popular food menu and great service. Accommodation is in en suite rooms, which ground floor and dog-friendly rooms, plus one with full disabled facilities.

The Yanwath Gate Inn
Yanwath, Penrith, Cumbria CA10 2LF
Tel: 01768 862386 • www.yanwathgate.com

The 'Yat' as it is fondly referred to, is a fine establishment with a restaurant featuring dishes prepared from locally sourced ingredients whenever possible. There is a carefully selected wine list and a good selection of real ales and draught beers.

The Oddfellows Arms
Caldbeck, Wigton, Cumbria CA7 8EA
Tel: 01697 478227 • Fax: 01697 478134 • www.oddfellows-caldbeck.co.uk

A delightful pub restaurant situated in the rural village of Caldbeck, offering accommodation and a wide range of mouth-watering dishes. Facilities include a jukebox, dart board, TV, and dominoes. 10 bedrooms are en suite, with coffee/tea making facilities.

Family-Friendly
Pubs, Inns & Hotels
See the Supplement on pages 177-178 for establishments which really welcome children

MIDDLE RUDDINGS Country Inn & Restaurant
Braithwaite, Keswick, Cumbria CA12 5RY

Located in the pretty Lakeland village of Braithwaite, two miles west of Keswick and opposite the impressive Skiddaw mountain range, Middle Ruddings was built in 1903, and is set in attractive gardens. Comfortable accommodation in six twins, six doubles and a single bedroom. An extensive menu is served in the Conservatory Dining Room with its superb views.

Tel: 017687 78436 • Fax: 01787 78438
e-mail: info@middle-ruddings.co.uk
www.middle-ruddings.co.uk

13 BEDROOMS, ALL WITH PRIVATE BATHROOM. ALL BEDROOMS NON-SMOKING. FREE HOUSE WITH REAL ALE. CHILDREN AND PETS WELCOME. BAR AND RESTAURANT MEALS. KESWICK 2 MILES. ££.

Barbon Inn
**Barbon,
Near Kirkby Lonsdale
Cumbria LA6 2LJ
Tel & Fax: 015242 76233**

If you are torn between the scenic delights of the Lake District and the Yorkshire Dales, then you can have the best of both worlds by making your base this friendly 17th century coaching inn nestling in the pretty village of Barbon.

Individually furnished bedrooms provide cosy accommodation, and for that extra touch of luxury enquire about the elegant mini-suite with its mahogany four-poster bed.

Fresh local produce is featured on the good value menus presented in the bar and restaurant, and the Sunday roast lunch with all the trimmings attracts patrons from near and far. A wide range of country pursuits can be enjoyed in the immediate area

Bedrooms, dining room and lounge non-smoking.

www.barbon-inn.co.uk

10 BEDROOMS, ALL WITH PRIVATE BATHROOM. ALL BEDROOMS NON-SMOKING. FREE HOUSE WITH REAL ALE. CHILDREN AND PETS WELCOME. BAR AND RESTAURANT MEALS. KIRKBY LONSDALE 3 MILES. S££££, D££££.

FREE or **REDUCED RATE** entry to Holiday Visits and Attractions – see our **READERS' OFFER VOUCHERS** on pages 179-204

Cumbria — NORTH WEST ENGLAND

**Near Sawrey, Ambleside LA22 0LF
Tel: 015394 36334
enquiries@towerbankarms.com**

Popular with tourists visiting Beatrix Potter's farmhouse, Hill Top, which adjoins the inn, this appealing cream and green hostelry is particularly recommended as somewhere where one can relax and savour the traditional country atmosphere.

A fine selection of Cumbrian real ales is always available, and food ranges from soup, freshly prepared sandwiches or Cumberland sausage and mash at lunchtimes to more substantial evening menus which feature local produce. Those wishing to indulge in Lakeland pursuits such as fishing (the inn has a licence for two rods a day on selected waters), walking, sailing and birdwatching will find delightful bedrooms, all en suite, with colour television and lovely views of the village.

www.towerbankarms.com

4 BEDROOMS, ALL EN SUITE. ALL BEDROOMS NON-SMOKING. FREE HOUSE WITH REAL ALE. CHILDREN AND PETS WELCOME. LUNCH AND DINNER AVAILABLE.
HAWKSHEAD 2 MILES. S£££users, D£££.

The Turk's Head

Market Square, Alston, Cumbria CA9 3HS • Tel: 01434 381148

For those in search of an olde world bar with the very best in draught beers and real ales – this is the place. Food is served in the lounge bar at the rear of the pub.

The Sportsman Inn

Compston Road, Ambleside, Cumbria LA22 9DR • Tel: 01539 432535

Set in the lovely village of Ambleside is this welcoming pub and lounge bar. Food is served throughout the day from an extensive menu of pub food favourites. There is an upstairs bar and a basement bar, where discos are regularly held.

A useful index of towns/counties appears on pages 205-206

THE EAGLE AND CHILD INN

Your No.1 choice for food and accommodation in the Lake District.

- Ideally placed for exploring the Lake District
- Local ales and regular guest beers
- 5 cosy en suite bedrooms, all with great views
- Excellent food from a varied menu
- Beer garden beside the River Kent

Kendal Road,
Staveley,
Cumbria LA8 9LP
01539 821320
info@eaglechildinn.co.uk
www.eaglechildinn.co.uk

5 BEDROOMS, ALL WITH PRIVATE BATHROOM. ALL BEDROOMS NON-SMOKING. FREE HOUSE WITH REAL ALE. CHILDREN WELCOME, PETS IN BAR ONLY. BAR AND RESTAURANT MEALS. DESIGNATED COVERED SMOKING AREA. WINDERMERE 4 MILES. S££, D££.

The Drunken Duck Inn
Barngates, Ambleside, Cumbria LA22 0NG
Tel: 015394 36347 • www.drunkenduckinn.co.uk

This restaurant inn is very lively in the evenings and is especially popular for its imaginative food menu, which is changed regularly. It has a charming beer garden – perfect during summer months.

The Owl & Pussycat

Hindpool Road, Barrow in Furness, Cumbria LA14 2NA • Tel: 01229 824334

A purpose-built pub with a stylish modern interior and a contemporary carvery offering excellent cuisine. There is an indoor play area where children can escape to, leaving mum and dad in peace!

Readers are requested to mention this FHG guide when seeking accommodation

Stan Laurel Inn

We are located close to the town centre and offer six changing cask ales, good quality home-cooked food, and comfortable accommodation.

We are situated on the southern tip of the Lake District, within easy reach of Windermere, Kendal and Coniston. The coast is only two miles away, and the area offers plenty of nice walks.

Good service, good food, good beer...what more could you ask for!

Stan Laurel Inn, 31 The Ellers, Ulverston LA12 0AB
Tel: 01229 582814 • e-mail: thestanlaurel@aol.com

Our website address is www.thestanlaurel.co.uk where further information on menus and pictures can be viewed.

3 BEDROOMS, 2 WITH PRIVATE BATHROOM. ALL BEDROOMS NON-SMOKING. FREE HOUSE WITH REAL ALES. CHILDREN AND PETS WELCOME. BAR MEALS.
BARROW-IN-FURNESS 8 MILES. S£, D£.

The Langstrath Country Inn
Stonethwaite, Borrowdale, Cumbria CA12 5XG
Tel: 01768 777239 • Fax: 01768 777015 • www.thelangstrath.com

A family-run retreat, ideal for ramblers and countryside enthusiasts, this beautiful inn was originally a miner's cottage but now boasts nine bedrooms with modern facilities. The cuisine is homemade and delicious, and food is served throughout the day. The downstairs lounge is welcoming, with an open fire and well stocked bar.

The Old Captain's House
Springfield Road, Bigrigg, Cumbria CA22 2TN • Tel: 01946 814392

The only pub in the village of Bigrigg, where food is sourced locally and is prepared from the freshest ingredients. Amenities include a dart and dominoes team as well as a pool table and jukebox.

BRIDGE INN (on facing page)

18 BEDROOMS, MOST EN SUITE. ALL BEDROOMS NON-SMOKING. JENNINGS HOUSE WITH REAL ALE. CHILDREN AND PETS WELCOME. BAR AND RESTAURANT MEALS. NON-SMOKING AREAS.
GOSFORTH 3 MILES. S££££, D££££.

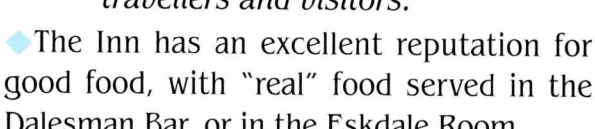

The Bridge Inn, once a coach halt, is now a fine, comfortable, award-winning country inn, offering hospitality to all travellers and visitors.

◆ The Inn has an excellent reputation for good food, with "real" food served in the Dalesman Bar, or in the Eskdale Room.

◆ We serve an excellent selection of Jennings and guest real ales.

◆ 16 en suite bedrooms. Four-poster Bridal Room.

◆ Weddings and other private and business functions catered for in our large function room with private bar facilities.

◆ Licensed for civil ceremonies, partnerships, naming ceremonies and renewal of vows.

◆ Dogs welcome in the bar and some bedrooms.

◆ Wi-Fi access and conference facilities.

10 minute drive to
"Britain's favourite view – Wastwater"
This unspoiled area of the Lake District offers superb walking and climbing.

Bridge Inn
Santon Bridge, Wasdale
Cumbria CA19 1UX
Tel: 019467 26221 • Fax: 019467 26026
info@santonbridgeinn.com
www.santonbridgeinn.com

The Wild Boar
Inn, Grill & Smokehouse

Nestling in a peaceful setting in the Gilpin Valley, the Wild Boar benefits from beautiful surrounding countryside, including its own private woodland and many other Lake District attractions close by. A special venue for many an occasion, whether that be a romantic or adventurous break, family get-together, intimate business meeting or as one of our very valued frequent diners. After undergoing a refurbishment the Wild Boar now offers individually designed bedrooms, Grill and Smokehouse with an open kitchen and chef's table. Adding a little more theatre to the dining experience.

THE WILD BOAR
CROOK, NEAR WINDERMERE
CUMBRIA LA23 3NF
RESERVATIONS: 08458 504604
www.elh.co.uk

English Lakes Hotels

WATERMILL INN & BREWING CO

Ings Village, Near Windermere LA8 9PY
Tel: 01539 821309
e-mail: info@lakelandpub.co.uk • www.lakelandpub.co.uk

CAMRA CUMBRIA PUB OF THE YEAR 2009

Named as one of the Guardian and Observer Best 200 Pubs in the Country 2009

- Up to 16 Real Ales. • Our own on-site Micro Brewery est. 2006.
- Viewing window into the brewery and beer cellar.
- Excellent range of food served 12 noon to 9pm every day.
- Varied menu and constantly changing Chef's Specials Board.
- 8 en suite bedrooms.
- Open all day every day except Christmas Day.
- Children and dogs most welcome.

8 BEDROOMS, ALL WITH PRIVATE BATHROOM. ALL BEDROOMS ARE NON SMOKING. REAL ALE. CHILDREN AND PETS WELCOME. BAR MEALS.
KENDAL 7 MILES.

The Beehive
Warwick Road, Carlisle, Cumbria CA1 1LH
Tel: 01228 549731 • Fax: 01228 510152

A John Barras pub located just a short distance from Carlisle city centre and close to Carlisle United Football Ground. The bar is well stocked well with draught beers and real ales, and live sporting fixtures are shown regularly on the big screen.

The Turf Tavern
New Market Road, Carlisle, Cumbria CA1 1JG • Tel: 01228 515367

Families enjoy the atmosphere at this Grade I Listed building, where a selection of delicious and affordable dishes is served throughout the day from a wide-ranging menu. The bar stocks a wide range of lagers, beers, wines and spirits, and there are two pool tables, a jukebox and Sky TV.

THE WILD BOAR (on facing page)

ALL BEDROOMS WITH PRIVATE BATHROOM. ALL BEDROOMS NON-SMOKING. REAL ALE. CHILDREN AND PETS WELCOME. BAR AND RESTAURANT MEALS.
WINDERMERE 3 MILES.

Lancashire

The Assheton Arms, Downham, Near Clitheroe BB7 4BJ

A delightful traditional country pub in a picturesque village in the beautiful Ribble Valley. Hosts, David and Wendy Busby offer a range of food to suit all tastes, specialising in seafood. There is a variety of modern and traditional beers; ample parking; patio for summer months. Children and dogs welcome. *Totally non-smoking.*

Tel: 01200 441227 • www.assheton-arms.co.uk

NO ACCOMMODATION. REAL ALES. CHILDREN AND PETS WELCOME.
BAR MEALS.
CLITHEROE 3 MILES.

The Waterside Inn
Twist Lane, Leigh, Lancashire WN7 4DB • Tel: 01942 605005

This Lancashire pub situated next to the canal was formerly a warehouse, and is an ideal place to come for a business lunch, or to catch up with friends over dinner or evening drinks. There is a beer garden to the side, and at the rear decking overlooks the canal.

Please mention **Pubs & Inns** of Britain when making enquiries about accommodation featured in these pages

THE FARMERS' ARMS (on facing page)

5 BEDROOMS, ALL WITH PRIVATE BATHROOM. ALL BEDROOMS NON SMOKING. ENTERPRISE INNS HOUSE WITH REAL ALE. CHILDREN WELCOME BAR AND RESTAURANT MEALS. NON-SMOKING AREAS.
CHORLEY 4 MILES. S££. D£££.

THE FARMERS' ARMS

Situated just two minutes from Jct 27 of the M6, The Farmers Arms is an ideal place to stay in the northwest of England, for visiting family and friends, business or indeed just pleasure.

The same welcome awaits you as it did the weary travellers who used the pub and its stables back in the 1700s. In those days the Farmers Arms was aptly named THE PLEASANT RETREAT and only found its new title of The Farmers in 1902. It has been on the estate of several brewing companies including Matthew Brown, Burtonwood, Duttons, and now is with your hosts, Malcolm and Ann Rothwell.

While still retaining its olde worlde charm, The Farmers continues to provide the very best of traditional cask ales and good hearty fayre. Sit back, enjoy and take in the warmth of this fine country inn.

All of our rooms have been designed to retain the olde worlde charm of The Farmers Arms, yet still meeting the requirements of today's discerning traveller. All rooms are en suite with tea and coffee making facilities and TV.

**Wood Lane, Heskin,
Near Chorley, Lancs PR7 5NP
Tel: 01257 451276
Fax: 01257 453958
www.farmersarms.co.uk**

★★★ INN

Greater Manchester

The Stamford Arms
The Firs, Bowdon, Altrincham, Greater Manchester WA14 2TW • Tel: 0161 9281536

A quintessential English pub standing opposite handsome St Mary's Church, with low-beamed ceilings and a spacious function room. With live sporting fixtures shown on big screens and high quality real ales, there's no reason not to drop in and stay for a while!

The Moss Trooper
Timperley, Altrincham, Greater Manchester WA15 6JU • Tel: 0161 9804610

The Moss Trooper is a CAMRA award-winning pub boasting a heated outdoor seating area, and a stylish interior with comfy sofas and inglenook fires. There is a cosy dining area with candlelit tables, plus an extensive range of wines, ales and beers.

The Old Pelican Inn
Manchester Road, West Timperley, Greater Manchester WA14 5NH
Tel: 0161 9627414 • Fax: 0161 9739144

Spacious 100-year-old inn located in West Timperley, popular with football supporters who enjoy watching live sporting fixtures over a pint of their favourite beer or ale. Food from the John Barras menu is available throughout the day.

The Cotton Kier
Watersmeeting Road, Bolton, Greater Manchester BL1 8TS
Tel: 01204 363010 Fax: 01204 559797

Situated on the outskirts of Bolton, this friendly family pub has a contemporary, light interior. The menu offers a wide choice of dishes, and entertainment comes in the form of a weekly quiz.

Scotland

The Ferry Boat Inn
Ullapool
Highlands
(page 150)

Kildrummy Inn
Kildrummy
Alford
Aberdeenshire
(page 137)

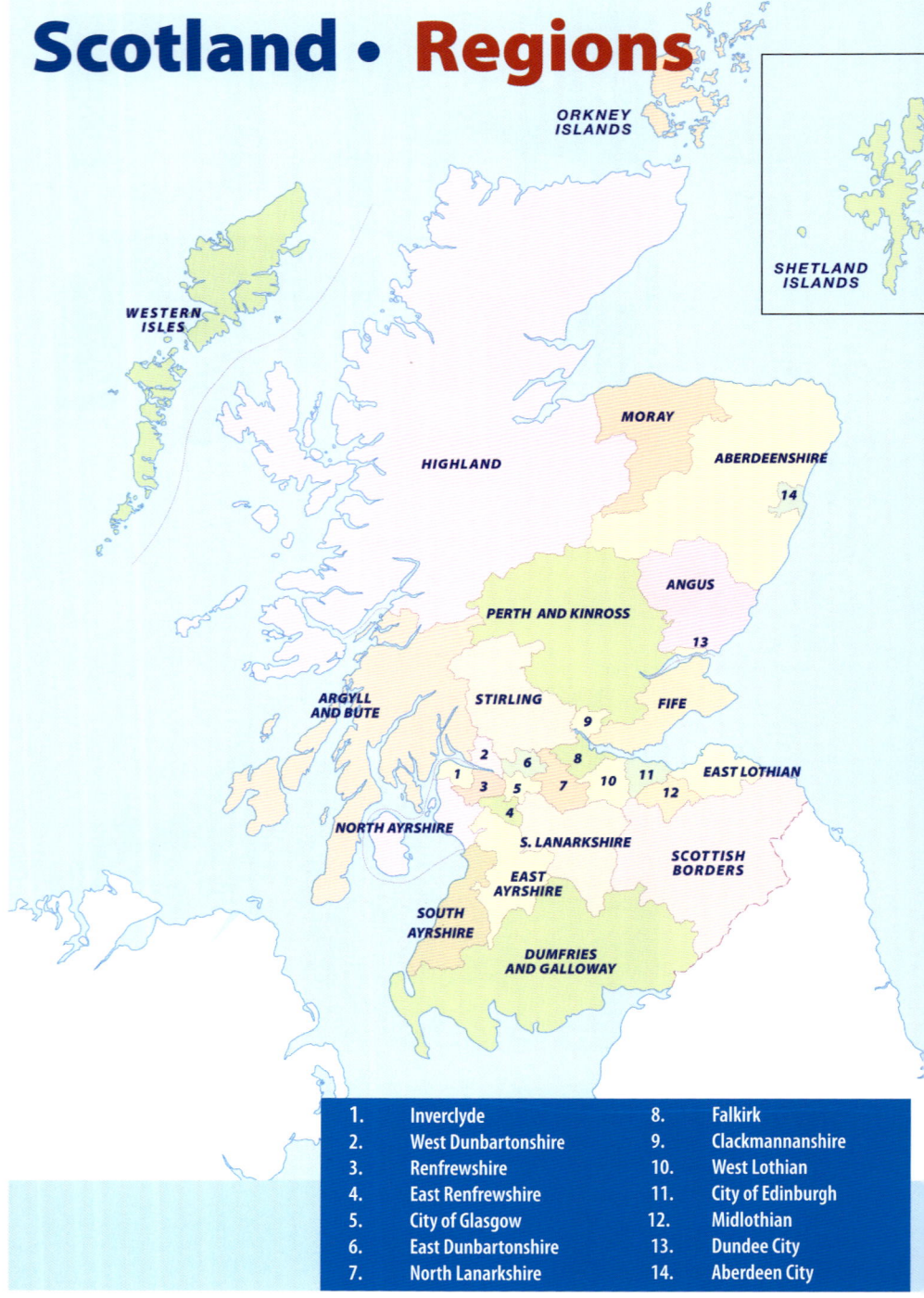

Aberdeen, Banff & Moray

KILDRUMMY INN • Kildrummy, Alford AB33 8QS
enquiries@kildrummyinn.co.uk • www.kildrummyinn.co.uk

- Located in the heart of rural Aberdeenshire, along the main A97, an excellent base for touring.
- All bedrooms are en suite, with tea/coffee making, radio alarm and TV.
- Superior quality cuisine is available in the comfortable Dining Rooms or in the relaxed atmosphere of the Sun Lounge.
- Separate guests' TV lounge.
- Ample parking.

Tel: 01975 571227

Local places of interest & activities include:
- Kildrummy Castle & Gardens • Huntly Castle • Golf Courses • Pony trekking
- Cycling • Hillwalking • Museums • Outdoor pursuits • Sporting Activities

4 BEDROOMS, ALL WITH PRIVATE BATHROOM. ALL BEDROOMS NON-SMOKING. FREE HOUSE WITH REAL ALE. CHILDREN WELCOME. RESTAURANT MEALS.
ALFORD 6½ MILES. S££, D££.

The Grays Inn
Greenfern Road, Aberdeen, Aberdeenshire AB16 5PY • Tel: 01224 690506
Newly furbished inn, with an open-plan kitchen for diners who like to watch their food being prepared. Live sporting fixtures are shown on big screens throughout the pub.

GRANT ARMS HOTEL
The Square, Monymusk, Inverurie AB51 7HJ
Tel: 01467 651226 • Fax: 01467 651494
e-mail: grantarmshotel@btconnect.com

This splendid former coaching inn of the 18th century has its own exclusive fishing rights on ten miles of the River Don, so it is hardly surprising that fresh salmon and trout are considered specialities of the restaurant, which is open nightly.

Bar food is available at lunchtimes and in the evenings, and a pleasing range of fare caters for all tastes.

12 double and twin rooms, all with private facilities, accommodate overnight visitors, and some ground floor bedrooms are available, two of which have been specifically designed for wheelchair users.

The hotel is centrally placed for enjoying outdoor activities and for attractions such as the Castle and Whisky Trails.

A traditional Scottish welcome and a real interest in the welfare of guests makes a stay here a particular pleasure.

SCOTLAND
Aberdeen, Banff & Moray

The Galley of Lorne Inn
Tel: 01852 500 284 ○ Ardfern, Argyll

Treat Yourself to some home comfort
Award-winning 17th Century Inn, near Oban
6 comfortable en-suite bedrooms
Free WiFi throughout the hotel
Cosy lounges & bars with log fires to unwind in
Lots to see & do, islands, castles, walks, fishing & golf
A warm friendly welcome awaits

Food & Drink delicious menus to savour
Lochview Restaurant & Sundeck
Homemade Mouthwatering Menu
Fresh local Lobster, Langoustines, Mussels & Scallops
Barbreck Farm Local Beef
Lunch Light Bites from £3.50, Kids Menu from £1.50
Real Ales, Perfectly Chilled Wines, Malt Selection

Call to Book
Quoting "Pubs & Inns", Reservations Essential

www.galleyoflorne.co.uk

6 BEDROOMS, ALL WITH PRIVATE BATHROOM. FREE HOUSE WITH REAL ALES. CHILDREN AND DOGS WELCOME. BAR AND RESTAURANT MEALS. NON-SMOKING AREAS.
LOCHGILPHEAD 12 MILES. S£££/££££, D£££/££££.

The Shepherd's Rest
Westhill, Aberdeen, Aberdeenshire AB32 6UF
Tel: 01224 740208 • Fax: 01224 745524

This inn is set in countryside surroundings on the way to Braemar, near Aberdeen. Secluded areas, a real fire and soft lighting will enhance your dining experience, and the adjacent Premier Inn provides 60 reasonably priced bedrooms.

THE SHIP INN
5 Shorehead, Stonehaven, Aberdeenshire AB39 2JY
Tel: 01569 762617 • www.shipinnstonehaven.com

Scottish bar serving a wide range of draught beers, real ales and 100 malt whiskies. The Captain's Table restaurant offers a range of home-cooked dishes prepared from fresh, locally sourced ingredients; food is also available in the bar. Accommodation is in eleven bedrooms, all with en suite shower, hairdryer, colour TV and harbour views!

GRANT ARMS HOTEL *(on facing page)*

12 BEDROOMS, ALL EN SUITE. ALL BEDROOMS NON SMOKING. FREE HOUSE WITH REAL ALE.
CHILDREN WELCOME. BAR MEALS, RESTAURANT EVENINGS ONLY.
INVERURIE 7 MILES. S££££, D£££.

Argyll & Bute

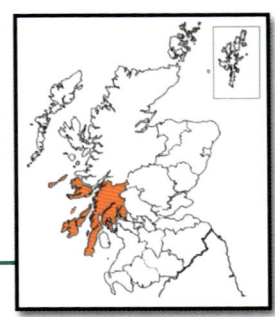

Cairndow Stagecoach Inn

A Warm Scottish Welcome on the Shores of Loch Fyne

**Cairndow, Argyll PA26 8BN
Tel: 01499 600286
Fax: 01499 600220**

Across the Arrochar Alps at the head of Loch Fyne, this historic coaching inn enjoys a perfect position. All bedrooms are en suite with TV, radio, central heating, tea/coffee and direct-dial phone. Seven de luxe bedrooms with king-size beds and five new lochside rooms are available. Dine by candlelight in our Stables Restaurant; bar meals and drinks served all day. Ideal centre for touring Western Highlands and Trossachs.

www.cairndowinn.com

Amenities include a loch-side beer garden, sauna, multi-gym, solarium; tee times are available at Loch Lomond.

SHORT BREAKS AVAILABLE

18 BEDROOMS, ALL WITH PRIVATE BATHROOM. ALL BEDROOMS NON-SMOKING. FREE HOUSE WITH REAL ALE. CHILDREN WELCOME. BAR AND RESTAURANT MEALS. NON-SMOKING AREAS.
ARROCHAR 12 MILES. S££, D££.

FHG Guides publish a large range of well-known accommodation guides. We will be happy to send you details or you can use the order form at the back of this book.

ARGYLL ARMS HOTEL (on facing page)

6 BEDROOMS, ALL WITH PRIVATE BATHROOM. ALL BEDROOMS NON-SMOKING. FREE HOUSE. CHILDREN WELCOME. BAR AND RESTAURANT MEALS.
TOBERMORY 50 MILES. S££, D££££.

The Argyll Arms Hotel, located on the waterfront of the village of Bunessan, and close to the ferry landing for the famous Isle of Iona, provides accommodation, bar and restaurant facilities on the beautiful Isle of Mull. With spectacular sea and island views, the hotel is the perfect base from which to explore the islands. Island tours available, wildlife watching day tours arranged. The new owners invite you to enjoy their friendly and relaxed Scottish hospitality in comfortable accommodation, value-for-money home cooked style food with many local ingredients, and the unique atmosphere of the Isle of Mull. Single, twin, double and family rooms available, all rooms recently refurbished, all en suite.

Make us your home whilst relaxing on the Isle of Mull.
Check out our website for full up-to-date information.

Open all day 365 days of the year catering for residents and non residents.
From £35.00 single. £60.00 double

Argyll Arms Hotel
Bunessan, Isle of Mull PA67 6DP
Tel: 01681 700240
e-mail: argyllarms@isleofmull.co.uk
www.isleofmull.co.uk

Craignure Inn
Craignure, Isle of Mull, Argyll, PA65 6AY

Craignure Inn is a small characteristic old drovers' inn providing excellent service, food and accommodation whether you're looking for a longer holiday, full of fun outdoor wildlife activities, or simply a relaxing short break for you and your family, partner or friend.

The main attractions of the island, Torosay Castle and its gardens, and Duart Castle with its Clan Maclean history, are at your doorstep. If you are lucky you might just see dolphins in Craignure Bay and otters just across the road by the rocks on the seashore. The Inn is open all year and prides itself on its friendly staff and warm welcome. It is favoured by locals and visitors alike.

There are three letting rooms, all en suite, with colour television and tea/coffee making facilities. The bar has a wide range of malts, fine wines, a large fire for the cooler evenings, outdoor seating and a cosy lounge.

There is an extensive bar menu with many wholesome, home cooked offerings using local produce such as Highland Beef, Hebridean Lamb, Mussels, Mull Cheddar and Smoked Trout.

We have regular live entertainment and welcome well behaved dogs. We provide information on local walks, trips and tours. Bus tours leave from Craignure, making it a great base for those without their own transport.

Craignure Inn
Isle of Mull, Argyll PA65 6AY
Tel: 016808 12305
craignureinn@btconnect.com
www.craignure-inn.co.uk

THE Coylet INN
Loch Eck, Argyll PA23 8SG

The Coylet Inn is one of Scotland's most enchanting 17th century coaching inns, ideally situated on the banks of Loch Eck. Its idyllic location makes it the perfect venue for a short break or romantic weekend away. The lovingly restored en suite bedrooms offer visitors comfort and a touch of luxury, while the good food, real ales, open log fires and stunning views make The Coylet the perfect country retreat. We now have a civil ceremony licence and tailored wedding packages are available.

www.coyletinn.co.uk
info@coyletinn.co.uk
Tel: 01369 840426

4 BEDROOMS, ALL WITH PRIVATE BATHROOM. FREE HOUSE WITH REAL ALE. CHILDREN WELCOME. BAR AND RESTAURANT MEALS. NON-SMOKING.
DUNOON 7 MILES. S££££, D££.

Argyll & Bute is a wonderfully unspoilt area, historically the heartland of Scotland and home to a wealth of fascinating wildlife. Here you may be lucky enough to catch a glimpse of an eagle, a wildcat or an osprey, or even a fine antlered stag. At every step the sea fringed landscape is steeped in history, from prehistoric sculpture at Kilmartin, to the elegant ducal home of the once feared Clan Campbell. There are also reminders of pre-historic times with Bronze Age cup-and-ring engravings, and standing stone circles. On the upper reaches of Loch Caolisport can be found St Columba's Cave, and more recent times are illustrated at the Auchindrain Highland Township south of Inveraray, a friendly little town with plenty to see, including the Jail, Wildlife Park and Maritime Museum. Bute is the most accessible of the west coast islands, and Rothesay is its main town. Explore the dungeons and grand hall of Rothesay Castle, or visit the fascinating Bute Museum. The town offers a full range of leisure facilities, including a fine swimming pool and superb golf course, and there are vast areas of parkland where youngsters can safely play.

CRAIGNURE INN (on facing page)

3 BEDROOMS, ALL WITH PRIVATE BATHROOM. FREE HOUSE.
CHILDREN AND PETS WELCOME. BAR MEALS. ALL PUBLIC AREAS NON-SMOKING.
TOBERMORY 18 MILES. S£££, D££.

Borders

SCOTLAND

The Black Bull, Lauder

18th Century Coachng Inn with 8 en suite bedrooms in period character with all modern amenities. Cosy bar, four dining areas. Just 20 minutes from Edinburgh, ideal for exploring Scottish Borders. Activities in the area include fishing, walking, golfing and places to visit.

The Black Bull Hotel, Market Place, Lauder TD2 6SR • Tel: 01578 722208
e-mail: enquiries@blackbull-lauder.com • www.blackbull-lauder.com

8 BEDROOMS, ALL WITH PRIVATE BATHROOM. ALL BEDROOMS NON-SMOKING. FREE HOUSE WITH REAL ALE. CHILDREN AND PETS WELCOME. BAR AND RESTAURANT MEALS. DESIGNATED COVERED SMOKING AREA. MELROSE 9 MILES. S££££, D££.

Covering about eighteen hundred miles, The Scottish Borders stretch from the rolling hills and moorland in the west, through gentler valleys to the rich agricultural plains of the east, and the rocky Berwickshire coastline with its secluded coves and picturesque fishing villages. Through the centre, tracing a silvery course from the hills to the sea, runs the River Tweed which provides some of the best fishing in Scotland. As well as fishing there is golf – 18 courses in all, riding or cycling and some of the best modern sports centres and swimming pools in the country. Friendly towns and charming villages are there to be discovered, while castles, abbeys, stately homes and museums illustrate the exciting and often bloody history of the area. It's this history which is commemorated in the Common Ridings and other local festivals, creating a colourful pageant much enjoyed by visitors and native Borderers alike.

Rates

S – SINGLE ROOM rate   D – Sharing DOUBLE/TWIN ROOM

S£ D£ = Under £35   S££ D££ = £36-£45   S£££ D£££ = £46-£55   S££££ D££££ = Over £55

This is meant as an indication only and does not show prices for Special Breaks, Weekends, etc. Guests are therefore advised to verify all prices on enquiring or booking.

Edinburgh & Lothians

Justinlees Inn
Dalhousie Road, Dalkeith, Midlothian EH22 3AT • Tel: 0131 663 2166

Prominently positioned on the roundabout in Dalkeith is this colossal white building with a beautifully traditional interior. With a circular centre bar and open plan layout, patrons may drink or dine where they choose. Amenities include free wifi, plasma screens, a large TV screen, pool table, dart board, and a beer garden.

IGLU (Bar & Ethical Eaterie)
2b Jamaica Street, Edinburgh, Midlothian EH3 6HH
Tel: 0131 476 5333 • www.theiglu.com/

Try food and drink from a different direction! Edinburgh is home to many fine establishments but none as special as this. Since the addition of a food service in 2005, its popularity has gone from strength to strength, offering all your favourite alcoholic beverages including cocktails.

THE MALT SHOVEL
11-15 Cockburn Street, Edinburgh, Lothians EH1 1BP • Tel: 0131-225 6843

This charming public house is located between the Royal Mile and the railway station. The interior is furnished in old dark wood, from the picture frames and fireplaces to the beams and flooring, with original stained glass on the doors. The pub boasts the biggest selection (105!) of malt whiskies in the area, plus well kept real ales. With haggis on the menu and live entertainment, this is definitely worth a visit!

The Shakespeare
65 Lothian Road, Edinburgh, Lothians EH1 2DJ • Tel: 0131-228 8400

The Shakespeare is one of Edinburgh's best-known and oldest pubs, and its location in the centre of the city means that it attracts a remarkably cosmopolitan crowd. Food is served throughout the day and live sporting fixtures are shown on an extra-large screen. Entertainment includes a weekly quiz and fortnightly karaoke.

The Rose Street Brewery
55 Rose Street, Edinburgh, Lothians EH2 2NH • Tel: 0131 2201227

The Rose was once a brewery, but is now a lively social centre on famous cobbled Rose Street in Edinburgh. Having undergone a recent refurbishment, the colour scheme is now an elegant blend of creams, browns and burgundy. Attractions include a great wine list and a range of dishes cooked to order – steaks are very popular here!

Hopetoun Inn
8 McDonald Road, Edinburgh, Lothians EH7 4LU
Tel: 0131-558 3523 • Fax: 0131-558 7538 • www.hopetouninn.co.uk

Regulars enjoy live sporting fixtures shown on a large screen, but that's not the only reason for coming to the Hopetoun. The facilities are great, with a pool table and dart boards, plus weekly entertainment such as a quiz, karaoke and live bands.

The Lady Nairne
228 Willowbrae Road, Edinburgh, Lothians EH8 7NG • Tel: 0131-661 3396

The perfect venue for a stag or hen weekend, The Lady Nairne is located just three miles from Edinburgh city centre. There is an extensive à la carte menu, with a good choice of wines as the perfect accompaniment. Accommodation is in 39 en suite bedrooms, all with modern facilities.

THE BALMWELL
39/41 Howden Hall Road, Edinburgh, Lothians EH16 6PG
Tel: 0131-672 1408 • Fax: 0131-666 1271

Lovers of wildlife can expect to see squirrels and foxes running about in the extensive gardens of this former convent. With a Two For One meal deals on delicious food and a wide range of wines from around the world, there's something for everyone.

The Cuddie Brae
Newcraighall, Edinburgh, Lothians EH21 8SG • Tel: 0131-657 1212

This Chef & Brewer pub venue is situated opposite the railway station, just five miles from the city centre. The interior is contemporary in style and the menu features mouth-watering dishes prepared from fresh ingredients. Accommodation is in 42 rooms, all en suite, with modern facilities.

The Granary
Almondvale Boulevard, Livingston, West Lothian EH54 6QN
Tel: 01506 410661 • Fax: 01506 415027

Purpose-built building located next to the Arndale Centre, offering great value for money and a comfortable environment in which to relax, dine and enjoy a glass of your favourite wine. The regulars are a friendly bunch who enjoy the weekly entertainment.

Fife

THE PEAT INN
RESTAURANT WITH ROOMS

Beautiful 5 Star restaurant with rooms situated just 6 miles from St Andrews in the village named after the Inn.

The restaurant has earned an international reputation over 30 years offering fresh Scottish produce, creativity and value, and is consistently voted one of the best restaurants in Scotland. A few steps away is 'The Residence', with 8 individual luxury suites, offering peace and comfort of the best of small country house hotels, but with a convivial and unpretentious atmosphere.

Peat Inn, by St Andrews, Fife KY15 5LH
Tel: 01334 840206 • Fax: 01334 840530
e-mail: stay@thepeatinn.co.uk
www.thepeatinn.co.uk

8 SUITES, ALL WITH PRIVATE BATHROOM. ALL BEDROOMS NON-SMOKING.
RESTAURANT MEALS.
ST ANDREWS 6 MILES. S££££, D££££.

Rates
S – SINGLE ROOM rate   D – Sharing DOUBLE/TWIN ROOM

S£ D£ = Under £35   S££ D££ = £36-£45   S£££ D£££ = £46-£55   S££££ D££££ = Over £55

This is meant as an indication only and does not show prices for Special Breaks, Weekends, etc.
Guests are therefore advised to verify all prices on enquiring or booking.

Highlands

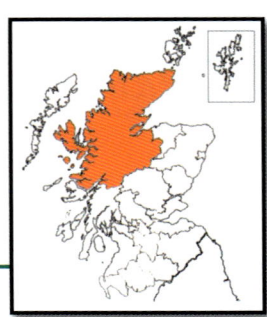

This former 19th century coaching inn on the John O'Groats peninsula is set in six acres of parkland, close to the Queen Mother's former Highland home, the Castle of Mey. Fully modernised, the hotel has eight centrally heated en suite bedrooms with colour television and tea making facilities; the spacious Pentland Suite offers a double and family room with en suite bathroom. Locally caught salmon, crab and other fine Highland produce feature on the varied table d'hôte and grill menus available in the Garden Room, while lighter meals and snacks can be enjoyed in the cosy Pentland Lounge. A warm Highland welcome awaits you.

THE CASTLE ARMS HOTEL Mey, By Thurso, Caithness KW14 8XH
Tel & Fax: 01847 851244 • e-mail: info@castlearms.co.uk

8 BEDROOMS, ALL WITH PRIVATE BATHROOM. ALL BEDROOMS NON-SMOKING. FREE HOUSE.
CHILDREN AND PETS WELCOME. BAR AND RESTAURANT MEALS.
JOHN O'GROATS 6 MILES. S££, D£.

Inn at Dalwhinnie
Dalwhinnie, Inverness-shire PH19 1AG
Tel: 01528 522257 • room@theinndalwhinnie.com • www.theinndalwhinnie.com

The Dalwhinnie provides guests with maximum comfort and offers lots of information on things to do and see. With live music and an abundance of traditional and modern fish dishes on the menu, it's an ideal spot to leave your troubles behind. All rooms are en suite and spacious with beautiful window views. Great selection of malt whiskies.

THE BEN NEVIS BAR
103 High Street, Fort William, Inverness-shire PH33 6DG • Tel: 01397 702295

Formerly this was the inn for the castle drovers; today, having undergone a contemporary makeover, the establishment exudes style and panache. The bar is split across two levels, with a restaurant upstairs affording stunning views. Enjoy a glass of fine wine on the new decking area overlooking the loch.

LAIRG HIGHLAND HOTEL (on facing page)

ALL BEDROOMS WITH PRIVATE BATHROOM.
CHILDREN WELCOME, PETS BY ARRANGEMENT.
GOLSPIE 17 MILES.

Lairg Highland Hotel

Lying in the centre of the village, Lairg Highland Hotel is an ideal base from which to tour the North of Scotland. Superb, home-cooked food, using the best local ingredients, is served in the elegant restaurant and in the attractive setting of the lounge bar. All meals can be complemented by a bottle of wine from a comprehensive list.

All bedrooms are individual in character, and furnished to a high standard, with en suite facilities, colour TV and tea/coffee hospitality tray.

The popular lounge bar, boasting some fine malt whiskies and good draught beers, is just the place to unwind and relax.

Main Street, Lairg, Sutherland IV27 4DB
Tel: 01549 402243 • Fax: 01549 402593
www.highland-hotel.co.uk • info@highland-hotel.co.uk

Among the many attractions of this scenic area are fishing, boating, sailing and golf, including Royal Dornoch nearby. Local places of interest include the Falls of Shin, Dunrobin Castle and Clynelish Distillery.

THE FERRY BOAT INN &

THE FRIGATE

We welcome you to The Ferry Boat Inn on the shorefront in Ullapool. All of our 9 bedrooms are en suite and we offer Bar Meals or fine dining in our beautiful Restaurant.

**Ferry Boat Inn
Shore Street
Ullapool IV26 2UJ
Tel: 01854 612 366
www.ferryboat-inn.com**

THE FRIGATE CAFÉ & BISTRO

High quality licensed Bistro, Café, Outside Caterers, Deli, Bakery and Take Away

Frigate Café, Shore Street,
Ullapool, IV26 2UJ
Tel: 01854 612 969
www.ullapoolcatering.co.uk

Perth & Kinross

**Glenearn House,
Perth Road, Crieff
PH7 3EQ
Tel: 01764 650111**

Yann's

at Glenearn House is a busy restaurant with rooms in Crieff, the gateway to the Highlands. The ambience is relaxed while the bistro has a real convivial atmosphere. The emphasis is on good food, kept simple and traditional, and featuring many bistro classics and a few Savoyard specialities.

We have five spacious bedrooms, all with en suite shower room or adjoining bathroom, and a large lounge where you can relax.

info@yannsatglenearnhouse.com
www.yannsatglenearnhouse.com

5 BEDROOMS, ALL WITH PRIVATE BATHROOM. ALL BEDROOMS NON-SMOKING. FREE HOUSE. CHILDREN AND PETS WELCOME. RESTAURANT MEALS WED-SUN.
PERTH 16 MILES. S£££, D££££.

THE FERRY BOAT INN (on facing page)

9 BEDROOMS, ALL WITH PRIVATE BATHROOM. REAL ALE. CHILDREN WELCOME. BAR AND RESTAURANT MEALS.
INVERNESS 55 MILES.

The Munro Inn
Strathyre, Perthshire FK18 8NA
Tel: 01877 384333

Traditional Highlands Inn set in beautiful Perthshire. Only an hour fron Edinburgh, Glasgow and Loch Lomond. Perfect base for walking, cycling, climbing, water sports, fishing or relaxing! Five different golf courses nearby. Great home cooking, lively bar, luxurious en suite bedrooms, drying room, broadband internet.

enquiries@munro-inn.com • www.munro-inn.com

9 BEDROOMS, ALL WITH PRIVATE BATHROOM. ALL BEDROOMS NON-SMOKING. FREE HOUSE WITH REAL ALE. CHILDREN WELCOME. BAR AND RESTAURANT MEALS.
CALLANDER 7 MILES. S££, D£££.

The Auld Bond
198 Dunkeld Road, Perth, Perthshire PH1 3GD • Tel: 01738 446079

This well-known public house is located on the western border of Perth, offering high quality food and ale. The Hungry Horse menu is simply bursting with choice and all the pub favourites are prepared from fresh ingredients. Facilities include an outdoor patio area, a children's play area, and a giant screen on which to watch the live sporting fixtures.

Perth & Kinross embraces both Highland and Lowland. Close to where the two Scotlands meet, a cluster of little resort towns has grown up: Crieff, Comrie, Dunkeld, Aberfeldy, and Pitlochry, set, some say, right in the very centre of Scotland. Perthshire touring is a special delight, as north-south hill roads drop into long loch-filled glens - Loch Rannoch, Loch Tay or Loch Earn, for example. No matter where you base yourself, from Kinross by Loch Leven to the south to Blairgowrie by the berryfields on the edge of Strathmore, you can be sure to find a string of interesting places to visit. If your tastes run to nature wild, rather than tamed in gardens, then Perthshire offers not only the delights of Caledonian pinewoods by Rannoch and the alpine flowers of the Lawers range, but also wildlife spectacle such as nesting ospreys at Loch of the Lowes by Dunkeld. There are viewing facilities by way of hides and telescopes by the lochside. Water is an important element in the Perthshire landscape, and it also plays a part in the activities choice. Angling and sailing are two of the 'mainstream' activities on offer, or enjoy a round of golf on any of Perthshire's 40 courses, including those at Gleneagles by Auchterarder.
The main town of Perth has plenty of shops with High Street names as well as specialist outlets selling everything from Scottish crafts to local pearls. With attractions including an excellent repertory theatre and a great choice of eating places, this is an ideal base to explore the true heartland of Scotland.

Stirling & The Trossachs

Behind The Wall
14 Melville Street, Falkirk, Stirlingshire FK1 1HZ
Tel: 01324633338 • www.behindthewall.co.uk

The radical way to live! Anything goes here at Behind The Wall, who proclaim that they 'make their own rules and then bend them'. This bar, eatery and entertainment venue is open all day and is ideal for the whole family, including young children. Facilities include an outdoor area and conservatory; wifi throughout.

The Rosebank
Main Street, Camelon, Falkirk, Stirlingshire FK1 4DS
Tel: 01324 611842 • Fax: 01324 617154

This prestigious Listed building is located in the small village of Camelon, beside the Forth and Clyde Canal between Edinburgh and Glasgow, and stands on the site of a former whisky distillery. Now a bar and 200-cover restaurant, it is ideal for a relaxing meal with friends or family.

The Outside Inn
Bellsdyke Road, Larbert, Stirlingshire FK5 4EG • Tel: 01324 579411

A newly refurbished inn, particularly popular with business people, shoppers and family diners. Original features include waterfalls and paths running through the indoor space; in summer, take advantage of the attractive beer garden. Facilities include wifi throughout and a smoking shelter.

Looking for holiday accommodation?
for details of hundreds of properties throughout the UK including comprehensive coverage of all areas of Scotland visit:
www.holidayguides.com

Scottish Islands

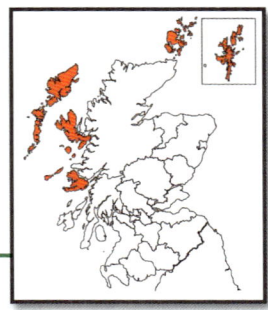

The Taversoe, Rousay, Orkney KW17 2PT • 01856 821325
www.taversoehotel.co.uk • careymaguire@taversoehotel.co.uk

Rousay, just 20 minutes' ferry crossing from the Orkney mainland, is a small friendly island graced with archaeological treasures, spectacular views and abundant wildlife. The Taversoe lies between the historic Tomb Trail and the renowned Westness Walk. Be as energetic as you like: walk, cycle or laze, unwind in a 'get away from it all' atmosphere.

- Rural location with panoramic sea views
- Accommodation available year round
- Friendly bar with games room • Private guest lounge
- A selection of local produce meals served daily
- Special diets catered for

3 BEDROOMS, 1 EN SUITE AND 2 WITH SHARED BATHROOM. ALL BEDROOMS NON-SMOKING.
BAR AND RESTAURANT MEALS.
ORKNEY 2 MILES (MAINLAND). S££, D£.

Other British holiday guides from FHG Guides

300 GREAT HOTELS

SHORT BREAK HOLIDAYS

The bestselling and original PETS WELCOME!

THE GOLF GUIDE - *Where to Stay, Where to Play*

500 GREAT PLACES TO STAY

SELF-CATERING HOLIDAYS • BED & BREAKFAST STOPS

CARAVAN & CAMPING HOLIDAYS • FAMILY BREAKS

Published annually: available in all good bookshops or direct from the publisher:
FHG Guides, Abbey Mill Business Centre, Seedhill, Paisley PA1 1TJ
Tel: 0141 887 0428 • Fax: 0141 889 7204
e-mail: admin@fhguides.co.uk • www.holidayguides.com

SCOTLAND
Scottish Islands 155

Since the 1700s this solid white-washed hotel has gazed over the Sound of Sleat to the Knoydart Mountains and the beautiful Sands of Morar, and as well as being one of the oldest coaching inns on the west coast, it is surely one of the most idyllically situated.

Not surprisingly, seafood features extensively on the menu here, together with local venison and other fine Scottish produce, and tasty bar lunches and suppers are offered as an alternative to the more formal cuisine served in the restaurant.

A private residents' lounge is furnished to the same high standard of comfort as the cosy guest rooms, all of which have private facilities.

ARDVASAR HOTEL
Ardvasar, Sleat, Isle of Skye IV45 8RS
Tel: 01471 844223 • Fax: 01471 844495
www.ardvasarhotel.com
e-mail: richard@ardvasar-hotel.demon.co.uk

10 BEDROOMS, ALL WITH PRIVATE BATHROOM. ALL BEDROOMS NON-SMOKING. FREE HOUSE WITH REAL ALE. CHILDREN AND PETS WELCOME. BAR MEALS AND RESTAURANT MEALS. BROADFORD 16 MILES. S£££££, D££££.

Rates

Normal Bed & Breakfast rate per person (single room)		Normal Bed & Breakfast rate per person (sharing double/twin room)	
PRICE RANGE	CATEGORY	PRICE RANGE	CATEGORY
Under £35	S£	Under £35	D£
£36-£45	S££	£36-£45	D££
£46-£55	S£££	£46-£55	D£££
Over £55	S££££	Over £55	D££££

This is meant as an indication only and does not show prices for Special Breaks, Weekends, etc. Guests are therefore advised to verify all prices on enquiring or booking.

Looking for Holiday Accommodation? then visit our website:
www.holidayguides.com

Search for holiday accommodation by region, location, type of accommodation (B&B, Self-Catering, Hotel etc)

Special requirements –
Are you looking for accommodation where children and pets are welcome, or maybe you want to be close to a golf course...

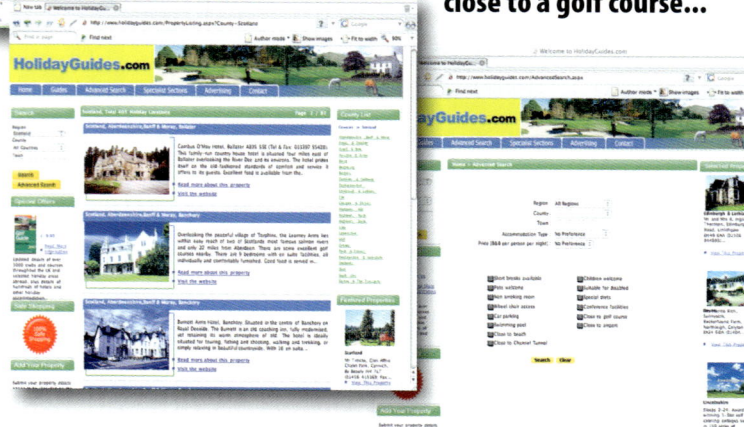

for details of hundreds of properties throughout the U

WALES

The Hand at Llanarmon
Ceiriog Valley
Near Llangollen
North Wales
(page 161)

Wales

Trewern Arms Hotel
Nevern
Newport
Pembrokeshire
(page 165)

Anglesey & Gwynedd

The Royal Ship Hotel
Queens Square, Dolgellau LL40 1AR

An early 19th century Coaching Inn, in the heart of the old market town of Dolgellau, ideally situated to explore the beauty of North and Mid Wales. Located in the Snowdonia National Park, one of the most picturesque countrysides imaginable, surrounded by mountains, rivers and fishing lakes, only a few minutes' drive to the coast of the Irish Sea, it is the perfect place for a relaxing holiday or short break. A family-run hotel, this historic building has been extensively modernised and extended over the years. Behind its attractive ivy-clad facade, 23 individual furnished bedrooms, bar and restaurant are on offer and provide our guests with the ideal atmosphere for a memorable stay.

Tel: 01341 422209 • Fax: 01341 424693
stay@royalshiphotel.co.uk • www.royalshiphotel.co.uk

23 BEDROOMS, 17 WITH PRIVATE BATHROOM. ALL BEDROOMS NON-SMOKING. ROBINSONS LTD HOUSE WITH REAL ALE. CHILDREN AND PETS WELCOME. BAR AND RESTAURANT MEALS.
BALA 17 MILES. S£££, D££.

The Antelope Inn
Holyhead Road, Bangor, Gwynedd LL57 2HZ
Tel: 01248 362162 • Fax: 01248 363710

This country inn offers stunning views of the Menai Straits. The interior has an open plan layout, with oak-beamed ceilings and comfortable seating. The restaurant has built up a reputation for serving fresh fish dishes from an adventurous specials board, plus a range of pub favourites. Attractions include a large beer garden and weekly quizzes.

FHG Guides publish a large range of well-known accommodation guides. We will be happy to send you details or you can use the order form at the back of this book.

Rates

S – SINGLE ROOM rate   D – Sharing DOUBLE/TWIN ROOM

S£ D£ = Under £35   S££ D££ = £36-£45   S£££ D£££ = £46-£55   S££££ D££££ = Over £55

This is meant as an indication only and does not show prices for Special Breaks, Weekends, etc.
Guests are therefore advised to verify all prices on enquiring or booking.

North Wales

The Halfway House
Church Street, Golftyn, Connahs Quay, North Wales CH5 4AS • Tel: 01244 819013

The Halfway House has recently undergone a major refurbishment and is now a stylish venue for the enjoyment of delicious food and well-kept beers and ales. The interior remains traditional and homely and facilities include a beer garden and a children's play area.

The White Horse Inn
The Square, Cilcain, Mold, North Wales CH7 5NN • Tel: 01352 740142

Located on the slope of Moel Fammau in North wales, an area of outstanding natural beauty. Homemade bar meals are prepared fresh to order, and the bar is stocked with a choice of real ales, draught beers, lagers and wines. The pub is especially popular with walkers, cyclists and horse riders. Children over 14 years welcome.

THE HARBOUR
Foryd Road, Rhyl, North Wales LL18 5BA • Tel: 01745 360644

The Harbour can be found just over the bridge in the little town of Rhyl. The building is attractively decorated inside and out, with comfortable fittings and furnishings, and the bar is well stocked with draught beers, spirits, ales and wines. Sample one of the pub's hearty meals which are available at most reasonable prices.

FREE or **REDUCED RATE** entry to Holiday Visits and Attractions – see our **READERS' OFFER VOUCHERS** on pages 179-204

THE HAWK & BUCKLE INN *(on following page)*
10 BEDROOMS, ALL WITH PRIVATE BATHROOM. FREE HOUSE WITH REAL ALE. CHILDREN WELCOME, PETS BY ARRANGEMENT. BAR AND RESTAURANT MEALS. DENBIGH 5 MILES.

The Hawk & Buckle Inn

Llannefydd, Denbigh,
Denbighshire LL16 5ED
Tel: 01745 540249

This 17th century coaching inn, recently under new management and with extensive renovation throughout, is located on the old stagecoach route to Holyhead between Denbigh and Abergele. Llannefydd is a peaceful, unspoilt village sitting high in the hills. This spot 200m above sea level looks out to beautiful views of the sea - on a clear day it is possible to see as far as Blackpool and the Cumbrian mountains.

The inn's black beamed lounge bar has undergone a complete renovation and transformation while retaining its character and charm, ideal if you want to take it easy after an invigorating countryside walk, while enjoying a wide range of fine wines, ales and spirits.

There is an extensive menu and where possible food is prepared from fresh, local ingredients; in addition to our usual evening menu we offer special Early Bird and Sunday lunch menus, and unique menus during the many special functions and themed nights the Inn holds.

The Hawk and Buckle also offers fine overnight accommodation in individually decorated and furnished en suite rooms, each of which has had complete renovation to reflect our desire for a cleaner, more elegant setting to complement the renovation in the rest of the building. Each bathroom includes a jacuzzi bath, shower and complimentary toiletries; one room has a double jacuzzi bath and complimentary bathrobes provided. TV and Internet access (via wireless) is available in each room.

> Guests may travel in any direction and be assured of interesting, scenic and charming places to visit. Whilst off the beaten track, the Inn is not far from the A55 which allows access to Snowdonia National Park, Llandudno, Betws-y-Coed, Bodnant Gardens and Chester, to name but a few. A member of staff will be happy to help you with suggestions for places to see during your stay as well as any events of interest during the tourist season, so please do not hesitate to ask.

e-mail: enquiries@hawkandbuckleinn.com
www.hawkandbuckleinn.com

The Hand at Llanarmon

Standing in the glorious and hidden Ceiriog Valley, The Hand at Llanarmon radiates charm and character. With 13 comfortable en suite bedrooms, roaring log fires, and fabulous food served with flair and generosity, this is a wonderful base for most country pursuits, or just relaxing in good company.

Tel: 01691 600666
e-mail: reception@thehandhotel.co.uk
www.TheHandHotel.co.uk

Llanarmon DC
Ceiriog Valley
Near Llangollen
North Wales
LL20 7LD

Carmarthenshire

The Prince of Wales Inn
Mynyddygarreg, Kidwelly, Carmarthenshire SA17 4RP • Tel: 01554 890522

This free house boasts six of its own real ales as well as several other Welsh ones and one real cider - all on tap! The size of the pub helps create a cosy, intimate ambience, with a log fire and interesting artefacts and memorabilia throughout.

The Phoenix
Penygroes Road, Gorslas, Llanelli, Carmarthenshire SA14 7LA • Tel: 01269 844438

The Phoenix is set in the rural village of Gorslas, a regular ramblers' haunt. The bar is stocked with a wide range of lagers, beers and wines and is the only public house in the village where food is served. The menu is imaginative and all dishes are prepared from fresh ingredients. Regular entertainment includes 60/70s nights, quiz nights and themed food evenings.

The Thomas Arms Hotel
Thomas Street, Llanelli, Carmarthenshire SA15 3JF • Tel: 01554 772043
www.thomasarms.co.uk

Having undergone a major refurbishment, this is the ideal spot for a relaxing drink after a hard day at work or for a family lunch or dinner. Accommodation is in ten en suite bedrooms with all modern facilities.

THE STRADEY ARMS
1 Stradey Road, Furnace, Llanelli, Carmarthenshire SA15 4ET
Tel: 01554 757968

For a quiet drink or meal, pop in to the Stradey Arms, located in the heart of the village of Furnace. Regular attractions include a weekly quiz, a large beer garden, a plasma screen and free wi-fi throughout.

THE HAND AT LLANARMON (on previous page)

13 BEDROOMS, ALL WITH PRIVATE BATHROOM. ALL BEDROOMS NON-SMOKING. FREE HOUSE WITH REAL ALE. CHILDREN AND PETS WELCOME. BAR AND RESTAURANT MEALS.
LLANGOLLEN 10 MILES. S£££, D££.

Ceredigion

The Ship Inn
Tresaith, Cardigan, Ceredigion SA43 2JL • Tel: 01239 811816
www.shiptresaith.com

Tresaith is a quaint little coastal village with popular beaches and one pub - the Ship Inn. Patrons can relax and enjoy the stunning views of the sea, and food is served throughout the day at reasonable prices. Accommodation is in four en suite rooms with colour TV.

The Black Lion Hotel
Pontrhydfendigaid, Ystrad Meurig, Ceredigion SY25 6BE
Tel: 01974 831624 • Fax: 01974 831052 • www.blacklionhotel.co.uk

Located only 20 minutes from Aberystwyth is this cosy, comfortable pub hotel, ideal for a walking holiday, with many walkways, cycle paths and nature trails to explore. There is a stylish bar and restuarant, plus five en suite bedrooms, each with modern facilities.

THE THREE HORSESHOES INN
Llangeitho, Tregaron, Ceredigion SY25 6TW • Tel: 01974 821244

Set in the rural heart of West Wales is this family-run pub with a large beer garden, a games room and a takeaway food service. All dishes are home-made and prepared from fresh ingredients. The bar offers a good selection of ales, draught beers and fine wines.

The Lord Beechings
Alexandra Road, Aberystwyth, Ceredigion ST23 1LE • Tel: 01970 625069

Aberystwyth is a university town and this large pub venue is a student favourite. Order food at the contemporary bar and relax with a pint of guest ale in a comfy chair while it is cooked to your liking. Facilities include free wi-fi.

Pembrokeshire

The Dial Inn is situated in Lamphey village, two miles east of Pembroke, and only a stone's throw from the Bishop's Palace.

THE DIAL INN
Ridgeway Road, Lamphey, Pembroke, Pembrokeshire SA71 5NU
Tel: 01646 672426
e-mail: dialinn@btconnect.com

This elegant, interesting and deceptively large village pub has excellent bar food, a daily blackboard menu, and an imaginative dining room menu.

All food is freshly prepared and cooked.

Also available are fine wines and cask-conditioned ales, and the inn is open for coffee, lunch, dinner and bar meals.

It is listed in all the best food and beer guides including 'Which?' and the AA. CAMRA.

5 BEDROOMS, ALL WITH PRIVATE BATHROOM. FREE HOUSE WITH REAL ALE. CHILDREN WELCOME. BAR AND RESTAURANT MEALS. NON-SMOKING AREAS. PEMBROKE 2 MILES. S££££, D££££.

FREE or **REDUCED RATE** entry to Holiday Visits and Attractions – see our **READERS' OFFER VOUCHERS** on pages 179-204

TREWERN ARMS HOTEL (on facing page)

10 BEDROOMS, ALL WITH PRIVATE BATHROOM. ALL BEDROOMS NON-SMOKING. FREE HOUSE WITH REAL ALE. CHILDREN WELCOME. BAR MEALS, RESTAURANT EVENINGS ONLY. NEWPORT 2 MILES. S£££, D£££.

TREWERN ARMS HOTEL

Nevern, Newport, Pembrokeshire SA42 0NB
Tel: 01239 820395 • Fax: 01239 820173

www.trewernarms.com
e-mail: info@trewern-arms-pembrokeshire.co.uk

Set deep in a forested and secluded valley on the banks of the River Nevern, this picturesque, 16th century hostelry has a warmth of welcome that is immediately apparent in the interestingly-shaped Brew House Bar with its original flagstone floors, stone walls, old settles and beams decorated with an accumulated collection of bric-a-brac. Bar meals are served here from a popular grill area. By contrast, the Lounge Bar is furnished on cottage lines and the fine restaurant has received many accolades from far and wide for its culinary delights.

The tranquil village of Nevern is ideally placed for Pembrokeshire's historic sites and uncrowded, sandy beaches and the accommodation offered at this recommended retreat is in the multi-starred class.

Powys

Llanymynech, Powys SY22 6EJ

Set in the historic village of Llanymynech, this former coaching inn has been renovated and upgraded to a very high standard. There are 5 superb bedrooms, all en suite, with tea/coffee making facilities and colour TV.

High quality home-cooked cuisine using local produce is served in the conservatory or more formal restaurant.

Situated in an area of outstanding natural beauty on the English/Welsh border, the hotel is an ideal base for walking on the nearby Offa's Dyke Trail and for exploring this historic area.

Tel: 01691 830582 • Fax: 01691 839009
e-mail: catelou@tesco.net • www.bradfordarmshotel.com

5 BEDROOMS, ALL WITH PRIVATE BATHROOM. FREE HOUSE WITH REAL ALE. ALL BEDROOMS NON-SMOKING. CHILDREN AND PETS WELCOME. BAR AND RESTAURANT MEALS.
OSWESTRY 6 MILES. S££, D£.

A useful index of towns/counties appears at the back of this book

BASKERVILLE ARMS HOTEL (on facing page)

13 BEDROOMS, ALL WITH PRIVATE BATHROOM. ALL BEDROOMS NON-SMOKING. FREE HOUSE WITH REAL ALE. CHILDREN AND PETS WELCOME. BAR AND RESTAURANT MEALS.
BRECON 17 MILES. S££, D££.

BASKERVILLE ARMS HOTEL

Delightfully placed in the upper reaches of the Wye Valley with the Black Mountains and Brecon Beacons on the doorstep, this comfortable retreat could not be better placed for lovers of both lush and wild unspoilt scenery. Hay-on-Wye, the 'town of books' is only 1.2 miles away with its narrow streets, antique shops and over 30 bookshops.

Run by resident proprietors, June and David, the hotel provides tasty, home-cooked food in bar and restaurant, using the best local produce.

With so many pursuits to enjoy in the area, this little hotel is a fine holiday base and well-appointed en suite bedrooms serve the purpose excellently. Totally non-smoking.

Single from £45, Double/Twin from £42.
See website for Special Rate Breaks.

**Clyro, Near Hay-on-Wye,
Herefordshire HR3 5RZ
Tel: 01497 820670
e-mail: info@baskervillearms.co.uk
www.baskervillearms.co.uk**

South Wales

HALF MOON INN
Llanthony, Abergavenny, Monmouthshire NP7 7NN
Tel: 01873 890611

Set amidst the beautiful scenery of the Vale of Ewyas and dominated by the slopes of the Black Mountains, this attractive inn on the winding B4423 is a welcome sight. Inside, a bar virtually unchanged over the years confirms the welcome, serving traditional ales, cider and good food.
In an area popular with enthusiastic ramblers and hill walkers, this is a favourite port of call, the boot and drying room being much appreciated. Close by are the fascinating remains of 12th century Llanthony Priory and a partly ruined 19th century monastery, with several Norman border castles within easy reach.
The Offa's Dyke and Beacons Way footpaths are only ½ mile away.
Wholesome B&B accommodation is available (single, double and family rooms).

e-mail: halfmoon@llanthony.wanadoo.co.uk
www.halfmoon-llanthony.co.uk

11 BEDROOMS, ALL WITH WASHBASINS. ALL BEDROOMS NON-SMOKING. FREE HOUSE WITH REAL ALE. CHILDREN AND PETS WELCOME. BAR MEALS.
HAY-ON-WYE 12 MILES, HEREFORD 16 MILES. S£, D£.

Rates
S – SINGLE ROOM rate   D – Sharing DOUBLE/TWIN ROOM

S£ D£ = Under £35   S££ D££ = £36-£45   S£££ D£££ = £46-£55   S££££ D££££ = Over £55

This is meant as an indication only and does not show prices for Special Breaks, Weekends, etc. Guests are therefore advised to verify all prices on enquiring or booking.

Ireland

Hunter's Hotel

Failte Ireland ★★★ • **AA** ★★★ **and Rosette**

Hunter's Hotel, the oldest coaching inn in Ireland, is located 45 minutes by car from Dublin City and 30 minutes from the ferry at Dun Laoghaire. It is set in two acres of award-winning gardens on the banks of the River Vartry. 16 bedrooms, all with private bathroom, colour TV and telephone.

Local amenities include fifteen 18-hole golf courses within a half hour's drive, notably Druid's Glen and The European.

The Gelletlie Family • Hunter's Hotel
Newrath Bridge, Rathnew,
Co. Wicklow, Ireland
Tel: +353 (0)404 40106 • Fax: +353 (0)404 40338
e-mail: reception@hunters.ie • www.hunters.ie

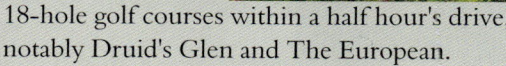

16 BEDROOMS, ALL WITH PRIVATE BATHROOM. ALL BEDROOMS NON-SMOKING.
BAR AND RESTAURANT MEALS.
WICKLOW 2 MILES.

Looking for holiday accommodation?

for details of hundreds of properties throughout the UK visit:

www.holidayguides.com

Pet-Friendly Pubs
A selection of Pubs and Inns where pets are especially welcome!

The Beehive
Waltham Road, White Waltham, Maidenhead SL6 3SH
01628 822871 • e-mail: beehivepub@aol.com • www.thebeehive-pub.com

Large front and back gardens. Bar and restaurant. Wheelchair facilities. Food served all day Saturday and Sunday. Pets welcome in gardens and bar area. Water bowls and treats for well behaved dogs.
Pet Regulars: Coco (Staffie), Bubbles and Ufano (the Guinness- drinking dog).

The Springer Spaniel
Treburley, near Launceston, Cornwall PL15 9NS
Tel: 01579 370424 • e-mail: enquiries@thespringerspaniel.org.uk
www.thespringerspaniel.org.uk

Country pub providing a warm welcome and specialising in home cooked, fresh, locally sourced food. Emphasis upon game, with beef and lamb from the owner's organic farm. Dogs can snooze by the fire or lounge in the beer garden - water provided
Pet Regulars: some very regular customers and their accompanying owners.

Cumberland Inn   Tel: 01434 381875
Townfoot, Alston, Cumbria CA9 3HX
stay@cumberlandinnalston.com • www.cumberlandinnalston.com

A comfy retreat in the secluded North Pennines. Real beer, real fires and real hospitality await your arrival. Home-made hearty fare available all day to revive flagging spirits. Our 5 recently refurbished rooms are all en suite. Muddy dogs and boots welcome.
Dog bowls filled with water (or even beer).
Pets welcome in bedrooms and bar. No charge for pets.

The Kings Arms Hotel
The Square, Hawkshead, Ambleside LA22 0NZ
Tel: 015394 36372
info@kingsarmshawkshead.co.uk • www.kingsarmshawkshead.co.uk

Family run, traditional Lakeland inn offering AA ★★★ Bed & Breakfast accommodation. Special mid-week rates. Quality home cooked food. Free fishing and 2 for 1 golf deals for guests. Children welcome.
Pets allowed in all areas except the dining room and kitchen.

Woolpack Inn
Eskdale, Cumbria CA19 1TH • 019467 23230
e-mail: office@greendoor.me • www.woolpack.co.uk

Free House situated in the heart of the breathtaking Eskdale Valley. B&B from £35pppn. Wide selection of real ales. Delicious food served all day.
Pets Facilities: Pets welcome throughout, including bedrooms.

The Coledale Inn
Braithwaite, Near Keswick, Cumbria CA12 5TN
Tel: 017687 78272
e-mail: info@coledale-inn.co.uk • www.coledale-inn.co.uk

Friendly, family-run Victorian inn in peaceful location. Ideally situated for touring and walking direct from the hotel grounds. Fine selection of wines and local real ales. Families and pets welcome.

Barbon Inn
Barbon, Near Kirkby Lonsdale, Cumbria LA6 2LJ Tel: 015242 76233
Friendly 17th century Coaching Inn with 10 bedrooms.
Country pursuits within the immediate area.
Nestling in Lune Valley between Lake District & Yorkshire Dales.
Large field beyond car park to exercise in.
Pet Regulars: our resident black Lab bitch – TESS
www.barbon-inn.co.uk

The Mortal Man Inn
Troutbeck, Windermere, Cumbria LA23 1PL
Tel: 01539 433193 • Fax: 01539 431261 • www.themortalman.co.uk

Quality real ales, carefully selected wines, cosy bedrooms with modern facilities, and cuisine prepared from fresh, locally sourced ingredients wherever possible, all in a delightful spot in the Troutbeck Valley.

THE HOOPS INN & COUNTRY HOTEL
Horns Cross, Near Clovelly, Bideford, Devon EX39 5DL
Tel: 01237 451222 • Fax: 01237 451247
sales@hoopsinn.co.uk   www.hoopsinn.co.uk

Thatched country inn with open log fires. All bedrooms en suite. Splendid base for touring and outdoor pursuits. Dartmoor and Exmoor within easy reach.
Pet Residents: Sky and Scout (Black Labs)

PORT LIGHT Hotel, Restaurant & Inn
Bolberry Down, Malborough, Near Salcombe, Devon TQ7 3DY
Tel: (01548) 561384 or (07970) 859992 • Sean & Hazel Hassall
e-mail: info@portlight.co.uk • www.portlight.co.uk

Luxury en suite rooms, easy access onto the gardens. Close to secluded sandy cove (dogs permitted). No charge for pets which are most welcome throughout the hotel. Outstanding food and service. Winner 2004 "Dogs Trust" Best Pet Hotel in England. Self-catering cottages also available.
Pets may dine in bar area • Pet food fridge available

172 PET-FRIENDLY PUBS & INNS

The Maltsters Arms
Tuckenhay, Devon TQ9 7EQ • 01803 732350
e-mail: pub@tuckenhay.demon.co.uk • www.tuckenhay.com

Bar food served daily at lunchtimes and evenings. Separate restaurant. Accommodation available. Barbecue at quayside during summer

Pets Facilities: pets welcome in public rooms and bedrooms. Dog biscuits available in bars.
Pets Regulars: Harvey, Bodie, Wellington and Biggles.

Julie and Shaun invite you to The Trout & Tipple, a quiet pub just a mile outside Tavistock, with a keen following for its real ale, (locally brewed Jail Ale and Teignworthy), real food and real welcome. It is a family-friendly pub – children are welcome – with a games room, patio area, dining room and a large car park. Traditional pub fare is served, with trout from the Tavistock Trout Fishery featuring on the menu; Sunday roasts are very popular.
Dogs welcome, bowls of water and treats available on request.

Parkwood Road, Tavistock Devon PL19 0JS
Tel: 01822 618886
www.troutandtipple.co.uk

The Trout & Tipple

The Fisherman's Haunt
Salisbury Road, Winkton, Christchurch, Dorset BH23 7AS
Tel: 01202 477283

Traditional coaching inn with 12 stylishly furnished bedrooms, some adapted for disabled access. Good food, wine and Fuller's cask ales. Close to Bournemouth Airport and many places of interest. Pets welcome.
Pets allowed in main bar and lounge for dining.
Two pet-friendly rooms in accommodation block.

www.fullershotels.com

The Brewers Arms
Martinstown, Dorchester, Dorset DT2 9LB • 01305 889361
e-mail: jackie_smith54@hotmail.com • www.thebrewersarms.com

Country pub with a lovely garden. Pub food. Amenities include a skittle alley, big car park and a large grassed area (which may be suitable for tents).
Chews, water bowls and areas out of the sun
Area in the pub where customers can eat and sit with their dogs.
Pet residents: Jodie and Poppy (both lurchers)

The Gaggle of Geese
Buckland Newton, Dorchester, Dorset DT2 7BS
01300 345249 • www.thegaggle.co.uk

Large pub with skittle alley, five acres of land including an orchard. Everything on our menu we make ourselves and as much of it is as locally sourced and seasonal as possible.

Pets welcome throughout • Water/food; fire in winter

PET-FRIENDLY PUBS & INNS

The White Swan
The Square, 31 High Street, Swanage, Dorset BH19 2LJ • 01929 423804
e-mail: info@whiteswanswanage.co.uk • www.whiteswanswanage.co.uk

A pub with a warm and friendly atmosphere, three minutes from the beach. Traditional pub food, Sunday roasts. Large beer garden. En suite accommodation with parking. Free wifi and internet access. TV and pool table. Children and dogs welcome.
Water, treats • Dogs allowed in beer garden, bar area and accommodation.
Pet resident: Bagsy (Sharpei). Regulars: Liddy and Em (Black Labradors), Sally and Sophie (Jack Russells), Patch (Jack Russell), Prince (King Charles Spaniel).

The Silent Woman Inn
Bere Road, Coldharbour, Wareham, Dorset BH20 7PA
Tel: 01929 552909 • www.thesilentwoman.co.uk

Traditional country inn nestling in the heart of Wareham Forest. Beautiful gardens, log fires in winter. All fresh ingredients, wonderful food. Real ales, good wines. Adults-only inside.
Water bowls and treats - and affection • Dogs allowed in bar areas and all outside areas except children's play areas.
Pet Residents: Rosie and Ellie (Labs). Regulars: Bruno, Tilly and many others.

The Whalebone Freehouse
http://whaleboneinn.sm4.biz/
Chapel Road, Fingringhoe, Colchester, Essex CO5 7BG
Tel/Fax: 01206 729307 • vicki@thewhaleboneinn.co.uk

Only minutes from Colchester, the Whalebone offers a wide range of excellent food and real ales. Pets are most welcome inside the pub and in the beer garden. Excellent dog-walking trails in and around Fingringhoe. Water bowls provided on request.
Pet Residents: Rosie and Poppy (Basset Hounds)

The White Buck • 01425 402264
www.fullershotels.com
Bisterne Close, Burley, Ringwood, Hampshire BH24 4AZ

Victorian Inn blending tradition with modern comfort, located in the heart of the New Forest, with 7 stylish bedrooms, excellent restaurant and bar. Play area and log trail available for children. Pets welcome.
Dogs are permitted in the bar area and bedrooms 1, 3 and 8 only.

BLACK HORSE INN
Pilgrims Way, Thurnham, Kent ME14 3LD
Tel: 01622 737185 • info@wellieboot.net • www.wellieboot.net

A homely and welcoming inn with its origins in the 18thC. The Black Horse is adorned with hops and beams, and has an open log fireplace to welcome you in winter. A separate annexe has 30 beautiful en suite bedrooms.
*Pets can stay in B&B rooms • Welcome in bar on lead
Dog bin and poop bags provided • Maps of local walks available.*

The Assheton Arms
Downham, Near Clitheroe, Lancashire BB7 4BJ
01200 441227 • www.assheton-arms.co.uk

Delightful, traditional country pub in picturesque village in the beautiful Ribble Valley. Range of food offered to suit all tastes. Variety of modern and traditional beers; ample parking; patio in summer months. Children welcome.
Pets Facilities: Pets welcome.

174 PET-FRIENDLY PUBS & INNS

The Inn at Whitewell • Forest of Bowland
Near Clitheroe, Lancs BB7 3AT • Tel: 01200 448222
reception@innatwhitewell.com • www.innatwhitewell.com

14thC inn in the beautiful Forest of Bowland.
7 miles fishing from our doorstep - trout, sea trout and salmon.
23 glamorous bedrooms, award-winning kitchen.
Voted by *The Independent* "One of the 50 Best UK Hotels"
Pets welcome in all areas except the kitchen!

Horse and Jockey
9 Chorlton Green, Manchester M21 9HS • 0161 860 7794
info@horseandjockeychorlton.com • www.horseandjockeychorlton.com

Traditional pub in village green setting. 6 cask ales, 50 bin wine cellar.
Disabled access. Traditional pub menu served all day, every day. Sunday lunch. Separate restaurant and function room.

Pets Facilities: all dogs get a biscuit, water bowl and lots of attention.
Pet Regulars: resident dog Eddie, Golden Labrador.

Stiffkey Red Lion   Tel: 01328 830552
44 Wells Road, Stiffkey, Norfolk NR23 1AJ
e-mail: redlion@stiffkey.com • www.stiffkey.com

5 ground floor en suite bedrooms, 5 on first floor;
all with their own external door.
Pets warmly welcomed

THE ROYAL OAK
Chart Lane South, Stonebridge, Dorking, Surrey RH5 4DJ
Tel: 01306 886420

Friendly country pub with traditional appeal. Range of food from quick bar snacks to full meals, using fresh local produce where possible.

Pets Facilities: enclosed garden at rear.
Pet Regulars: resident pub dog - Ho, Ziggy.

Visit the FHG website
www.holidayguides.com
for pet-friendly acccommodation around Britain

PET-FRIENDLY PUBS & INNS

The Bat and Ball
15 Bat and Ball Lane, Boundstone, Farnham GU10 4SA
Tel: 01252 792108
info@thebatandball.co.uk • www.thebatandball.co.uk

Traditional village pub. • Selection of 6 ales. • Extensive home made menu. • Garden and patio area. • Situated on five converging footpaths - ideal drop-in place for walkers. • Children's play area. • Pets on leads allowed in the pub.
Pet Regulars: Mac (Assistant Landlord)

Old Ship Inn
Uckfield Road, Ringmer, East Sussex BN8 5RP • 01273 814223
e-mail: info@oldshippub.co.uk • www.oldshippub.co.uk

On the A26 between Lewes and Uckfield, this family-run 17thC inn is the perfect place to relax, with food served from 12 to 9.30pm daily. The charming oak-beamed bar and restaurant is set in one acre of well tended, enclosed gardens. Well behaved dogs welcome inside.
Pet Resident: Marley (Bernese Mountain Dog)

The Fish House
Chilgrove, Chichester, West Sussex PO18 9HX • Tel 01243 519 444
bookings@thefishhouse.co.uk • www.thefishhouse.co.uk

Luxury overnight accommodation and culinary excellence, an oasis of sumptuous dining and self-indulgent relaxation on the outskirts of Chichester. Fifteen luxurious guest rooms and the finest in à la carte dining.

We accept well behaved pets.
You can dine with them in the Oyster Bar.

The Oak
Coventry Road, Baginton, Coventry CV8 3AU
Tel: 02476 518855 • Fax: 02476 518866
e-mail: thebagintonoak@aol.com • www.thebaginton.co.uk

Bed & Breakfast accommodation. Family friendly pub. Quality home cooked food. Pets welcome. Extensive exercise area. Water bowls available. Mobile grooming parlour and local dog walking service - details on request. *Pet Residents: Beau and Jasper (Border Collies)*

The Lamb Inn
High Street, Hindon, Wiltshire SP3 6DP
Tel: 01747 820573 • Fax: 01747 820605
www.lambathindon.co.uk

12th Century historic inn with bedrooms full of character.
Outstanding food and great wine selection.
Pets welcome in the bar and bedrooms. ETC/AA ★★★★

The Green Dragon
High Row, Exelby, Bedale DL8 2HA • 01677 422233
www.thegreendragonexelby.com

A family run, independent country inn taking pride in its friendly welcoming service, an excellent restaurant, comfortable, well appointed accommodation and a large car park.
There are four tastefully decorated rooms all en suite, with colour television and hospitality tray.

176 PET-FRIENDLY PUBS & INNS

Old Hall Inn
Tel: 01756 752441
Main Street, Threshfield, Grassington, N. Yorks BD23 5HB
oldhallinn@fsmail.net • www.oldhallinnandcottages.co.uk

18thC Inn, renowned for fine ales and award-winning cuisine. Large beer garden. Children's outdoor play area. B&B in four en suite bedrooms; quality self-catering available in adjacent cottages.
Well behaved dogs welcome.

The Harrogate Arms
Crag Lane, Harrogate HG3 1QA
Tel: 01423 567950
e-mail: info@theharrogatearms.com • www.theharrogatearms.com

An 18th century listed building set amid tranquil woodland. Restaurant and bar. Ideal for walkers. Children welcome. Pets welcome and permitted in bar and dining area. Dog bowl permanently available.

The Castle Inn
7 Wistowgate, Cawood
Selby, North Yorkshire YO8 3SH
Tel: 01757 268324
info@castleinncawood.co.uk • www.castleinncawood.co.uk

18thC village pub with a 60-seat restaurant and an 18-pitch caravan site. All food is local and fresh.
Pets Welcome • Water bowls outside.

ANNANDALE ARMS HOTEL
HIGH STREET, MOFFAT DG10 9HF
Tel: 01683 220013 • Fax: 01683 221395

A warm welcome is offered to dogs with well-mannered and house-trained owners. There are all the comforts and facilities that owners enjoy such as an excellent restaurant and a relaxing panelled bar. STB ★★★ Hotel.
www.annandalearmshotel.co.uk • pw@annandalearmshotel.co.uk

Other British holiday guides from FHG Guides

300 GREAT HOTELS • SHORT BREAK HOLIDAYS
The bestselling and original PETS WELCOME!
THE GOLF GUIDE - *Where to Play, Where to Stay*
500 GREAT PLACES TO STAY
SELF-CATERING HOLIDAYS • BED & BREAKFAST STOPS
CARAVAN & CAMPING HOLIDAYS • FAMILY BREAKS

Published annually: available in all good bookshops or direct from the publisher:
FHG Guides, Abbey Mill Business Centre, Seedhill, Paisley PA1 1TJ
Tel: 0141 887 0428 • Fax: 0141 889 7204
e-mail: admin@fhguides.co.uk • www.holidayguides.com

Family-Friendly Pubs & Inns

This is a selection of establishments which make an extra effort to cater for parents and children. The majority provide a separate children's menu or they may be willing to serve small portions of main course dishes on request; there are often separate outdoor or indoor play areas where the junior members of the family can let off steam while Mum and Dad unwind over a drink.

NB: Not all of the establishments featured here have a listing in the main section of this book.

- half portions
- children's menu
- garden or play area
- baby-changing facilities
- high chairs
- family room

THE GLOBE INN
Globe Lane, Stoke Road,
Old Linslade, Leighton Buzzard,
Bedfordshire LU7 2TA
Tel: 01525 373338
www.globeinn-leighton-buzzard.co.uk

CROOKED INN
Stoketon Cross, Trematon,
Saltash, Cornwall PL12 4RZ
Tel: 01752 848177
www.crooked-inn.co.uk

GREYHOUND HOTEL
Main Street, Shap, Penrith,
Cumbria CA10 3PW
Tel: 01931 716474
www.greyhoundshap.co.uk

EAGLE & CHILD INN
Kendal Road, Staveley,
Cumbria LA8 9LP
Tel: 01539 821320
www.eaglechildinn.co.uk

PORT LIGHT HOTEL,
Bolberry Down, Malborough,
Nr Salcombe, South Devon TQ7 3DY
Tel: 01548 561384
www.portlight.co.uk

FAMILY-FRIENDLY PUBS & INNS

THE CASTLE INN
Lulworth Cove
Dorset BH20 5RN
Tel: 01929 400311
www.lulworthinn.com

OLD PASSAGE
Passage Road, Arlingham,
Gloucestershire GL2 7JR
Tel: 01452 740547
www.theoldpassage.com

THE NEW INN
Mill Road, Shalfleet
Newport, Isle of Wight PO30 4NS
Tel: 01983 531314
www.thenew-inn.co.uk

HORSE & GROOM
Main Road, Ningwood
Isle of Wight PO30 4NW
Tel: 01983 760672
www.horse-and-groom.com

THE WINDMILL INN
Chatham Green, Nr Little Waltham
Chelmsford, Essex CM3 3LE
Tel: 01245 361188
www.windmillmotorinn.co.uk

THE MUNRO INN
Strathyre
Perthshire FK18 8NA
Tel: 01877 384333
www.munro-inn.com

YANN'S AT GLENEARN HOUSE
Perth Road, Crieff,
Perth & Kinross PH7 3EQ
Tel: 01764 650111
www.yannsatglenearnhouse.com

THE BRADFORD ARMS
Llanmynech, Powys SY22 6EJ
Tel: 01691 830582
www.bradfordarmshotel.com

179

READERS' OFFER 2011

LEIGHTON BUZZARD RAILWAY
Page's Park Station, Billington Road,
Leighton Buzzard, Bedfordshire LU7 4TN
Tel: 01525 373888
e-mail: station@lbngrs.org.uk
www.buzzrail.co.uk

One FREE adult/child with full-fare adult ticket
Valid 13/3/2011 - 30/10/2011

NOT TO BE USED IN CONJUNCTION WITH ANY OTHER OFFER

READERS' OFFER 2011

BEKONSCOT MODEL VILLAGE & RAILWAY
Warwick Road, Beaconsfield,
Buckinghamshire HP9 2PL
Tel: 01494 672919
e-mail: info@bekonscot.co.uk
www.bekonscot.co.uk

One child FREE when accompanied by full-paying adult
Valid February to October 2011

NOT TO BE USED IN CONJUNCTION WITH ANY OTHER OFFER

READERS' OFFER 2011

BUCKINGHAMSHIRE RAILWAY CENTRE
Quainton Road Station, Quainton,
Aylesbury HP22 4BY
Tel: 01296 655720
e-mail: office@bucksrailcentre.org
www.bucksrailcentre.org

One child FREE with each full-paying adult
Not valid for Special Events or Day Out with Thomas

NOT TO BE USED IN CONJUNCTION WITH ANY OTHER OFFER

READERS' OFFER 2011

NENE VALLEY RAILWAY
Wansford Station, Stibbington,
Peterborough, Cambs PE8 6LR
Tel: 01780 784444
e-mail: nvrorg@nvr.org.uk
www.nvr.org.uk

One child FREE with each full paying adult.
Valid Jan. to end Oct. 2011 (excludes galas and pre-ticketed events)

NOT TO BE USED IN CONJUNCTION WITH ANY OTHER OFFER

A 70-minute journey into the lost world of the English narrow gauge light railway. Features historic steam locomotives from many countries. **WELL BEHAVED PETS WELCOME**	**Open:** Sundays and Bank Holiday weekends 13 March to 30 October. Additional days in summer, and school holidays. **Directions:** on south side of Leighton Buzzard. Follow brown signs from town centre or A505/A4146 bypass.

FHG GUIDES, ABBEY MILL BUSINESS CENTRE, PAISLEY PA1 1TJ • www.holidayguides.com

Be a giant in a magical miniature world of make-believe depicting rural England in the 1930s. "A little piece of history that is forever England."	**Open:** 10am-5pm daily mid February to end October. **Directions:** Junction 16 M25, Junction 2 M40.

FHG GUIDES, ABBEY MILL BUSINESS CENTRE, PAISLEY PA1 1TJ • www.holidayguides.com

A working steam railway centre. Steam train rides, miniature railway rides, large collection of historic preserved steam locomotives, carriages and wagons.	**Open:** daily April to October 10.30am to 4.30pm. Variable programme - check website or call. **Directions:** off A41 Aylesbury to Bicester Road, 6 miles north west of Aylesbury.

FHG GUIDES, ABBEY MILL BUSINESS CENTRE, PAISLEY PA1 1TJ • www.holidayguides.com

Take a trip back in time on the delightful Nene Valley Railway with its heritage steam and diesel locomotives, There is a 7½ mile ride from Wansford to Peterborough via Yarwell, with shop, museum and excellent cafe at Wansford Station (free parking).	**Open:** please phone or see website for details. **Directions:** situated 4 miles north of Peterborough on the A1

FHG GUIDES, ABBEY MILL BUSINESS CENTRE, PAISLEY PA1 1TJ • www.holidayguides.com

THE RAPTOR FOUNDATION
The Heath, St Ives Road,
Woodhurst, Huntingdon, Cambs PE28 3BT
Tel: 01487 741140 • Fax: 01487 841140
e-mail: heleowl@aol.com
www.raptorfoundation.org.uk

FHG READERS' OFFER 2011

TWO for the price of ONE
Valid until end 2011 (not Bank Holidays)

NOT TO BE USED IN CONJUNCTION WITH ANY OTHER OFFER

CATALYST SCIENCE DISCOVERY CENTRE
Mersey Road, Widnes,
Cheshire WA8 0DF
Tel: 0151-420 1121 • Fax: 0808 280 0890
e-mail: info@catalyst.org.uk
www.catalyst.org.uk

FHG READERS' OFFER 2011

One child admitted FREE with one full paying adult.
Only one free admission per adult/ticket. No photocopies.

NOT TO BE USED IN CONJUNCTION WITH ANY OTHER OFFER

LAPPA VALLEY RAILWAY
Benny Halt, St Newlyn East,
Newquay, Cornwall TR8 5LX
Tel: 01872 510317
e-mail: info@lappavalley.co.uk
www.lappavalley.co.uk

FHG READERS' OFFER 2011

75p per person OFF up to a maximum of £3
Valid Easter to end October 2011.

NOT TO BE USED IN CONJUNCTION WITH ANY OTHER OFFER

PORFELL WILDLIFE PARK & SANCTUARY
Trecangate, Near Llanreath,
Liskeard,
Cornwall PL14 4RE
Tel: 01503 220211
www.porfellanimalland.co.uk

FHG READERS' OFFER 2011

One child FREE with one paying adult per voucher
Valid 1st April-31st October 2011.

NOT TO BE USED IN CONJUNCTION WITH ANY OTHER OFFER

Birds of Prey Centre offering audience participation in flying displays which are held 3 times daily. Tours, picnic area, gift shop, tearoom, craft shop.

Open: 10am-5pm all year except Christmas and New Year.

Directions: follow brown tourist signs from B1040.

Come and discover an interactive world of science and technology. Ride in the scenic glass lift to the rooftop observatory or visit Scientrific or Birth of and Industry galleries, home to over 50 hands-on exhibits. With holiday workshops, an interactive theatre, car parking, gift shop, cafe and playground, science has never been so much fun!!

Open: Tues-Fri 10am-5pm; Sat and Sun 11am-5pm. Closed 23-26 Dec and 31 Dec/Jan 1.

Directions: Junction 7 M62 or Junction 12 M56. Follow brown tourist signs.

Three miniature railways, plus leisure park with canoes, crazy golf, large children's play area with fort, brickpath maze, wooded walks (all inclusive). Dogs welcome (50p).

Open: Easter to end October

Directions: follow brown tourist signs from A30 and A3075

Porfell is home to wild and exotic animals from around the world. Idyllically situated amongst the rolling hills of south east Cornwall. It has a beautiful woodland with raised boardwalks over marsh areas, and a children's farm.

Open: 10am-6pm daily from April 1st to October 31st.

Directions: A38 Liskeard, A390 for St Austell. Turn off at East Taphouse on to B3359, follow brown tourist signs.

TAMAR VALLEY DONKEY PARK
St Ann's Chapel, Gunnislake,
Cornwall PL18 9HW
Tel: 01822 834072
e-mail: info@donkeypark.com
www.donkeypark.com

50p OFF per person, up to 6 persons
Valid from Easter until end October 2011

NOT TO BE USED IN CONJUNCTION WITH ANY OTHER OFFER

CARS OF THE STARS MOTOR MUSEUM
Standish Street, Keswick
Cumbria CA12 5LS
Tel: 017687 73757
e-mail: cotsmm@aol.com
www.carsofthestars.com

One FREE child with two paying adults
Valid during normal opening times.

NOT TO BE USED IN CONJUNCTION WITH ANY OTHER OFFER

THE BOND MUSEUM
Southey Hill, Keswick,
Cumbria CA12 5NR
Tel: 017687 75007
e-mail: thebondmuseum@aol.com
www.thebondmuseum.com

One FREE child with two paying adults.
Valid February to October 2011.

NOT TO BE USED IN CONJUNCTION WITH ANY OTHER OFFER

THE BEACON
West Strand, Whitehaven,
Cumbria CA28 7LY
Tel: 01946 592302 • Fax: 01946 598150
e-mail: thebeacon@copelandbc.gov.uk
www.thebeacon-whitehaven.co.uk

One FREE adult/concesssion when accompanied by one full paying
adult/concession. Under 16s free. Valid from Oct 2010 to end 2011.
Not valid for special events. Day tickets only.

NOT TO BE USED IN CONJUNCTION WITH ANY OTHER OFFER

Cornwall's only Donkey Sanctuary set in 14 acres overlooking the beautiful Tamar Valley. Donkey grooming, goat hill, children's playgrounds, cafe and picnic area. All-weather play barn.	**Open:** Easter to end Oct: daily 10am to 5pm. Nov to March: weekends and all school holidays 10.30am to 4.30pm **Directions:** just off A390 between Callington and Gunnislake at St Ann's Chapel.

FHG GUIDES, ABBEY MILL BUSINESS CENTRE, PAISLEY PA1 1TJ • www.holidayguides.com

This world famous motor museum features vehicles from TV and film - Chitty Chitty Bang Bang, Batmobiles, A-Team van, KITT and more. Also souvenir and autograph shop.	**Open:** 10am to 5pm February half term, and Easter to end November. Weekends only in December. **Directions:** M6 to Penrith, A66 to Keswick. Located in centre of town, by Bell Close car park.

FHG GUIDES, ABBEY MILL BUSINESS CENTRE, PAISLEY PA1 1TJ • www.holidayguides.com

For all "Bond" or car fans this is a must! Aston Martins, Lotus, even a T55 Russsian tank from the film "Goldeneye". New this year - Zao's Jaguar from "Die Another Day", and Aston Martin DBS from "Quantum of Solace". Cinema and shop.	**Open:** 10am to 5pm February to end October. **Directions:** from Penrith (M6) take A66 to Keswick. Free parking.

FHG GUIDES, ABBEY MILL BUSINESS CENTRE, PAISLEY PA1 1TJ • www.holidayguides.com

The Beacon is the Copeland area's interactive museum, tracing the area's rich history, from as far back as prehistoric times to the modern day. Enjoy panoramic views of the Georgian town and harbour from the 4th floor viewing gallery. Art gallery, gift shop, restaurant. Fully accessible.	**Open:** open all year (excl. 24-26 Dec) Tuesday to Sunday, plus Monday Bank Holidays. **Directions:** enter Whitehaven from north or south on A595. Follow the town centre and brown museum signs; located on harbourside.

FHG GUIDES, ABBEY MILL BUSINESS CENTRE, PAISLEY PA1 1TJ • www.holidayguides.com

READERS' OFFER 2011

CRICH TRAMWAY VILLAGE
Crich, Matlock
Derbyshire DE4 5DP
Tel: 01773 854321 • Fax: 01773 854320
e-mail: enquiry@tramway.co.uk
www.tramway.co.uk

One child FREE with every full-paying adult
Valid during 2011

NOT TO BE USED IN CONJUNCTION WITH ANY OTHER OFFER

READERS' OFFER 2011

THE MILKY WAY ADVENTURE PARK
The Milky Way, Clovelly,
Bideford, Devon EX39 5RY
Tel: 01237 431255
e-mail: info@themilkyway.co.uk
www.themilkyway.co.uk

10% discount on entrance charge.
Valid Easter to end October (not August).

NOT TO BE USED IN CONJUNCTION WITH ANY OTHER OFFER

READERS' OFFER 2011

THE BIG SHEEP
Abbotsham, Bideford,
North Devon EX39 5AP
Tel: 01237 472366 • Fax: 01237 477916
e-mail: info@thebigsheep.co.uk
www.thebigsheep.co.uk

£1 OFF per person up to £5.

NOT TO BE USED IN CONJUNCTION WITH ANY OTHER OFFER

READERS' OFFER 2011

DEVONSHIRE COLLECTION OF PERIOD COSTUME
Totnes Costume Museum,
Bogan House, 43 High Street,
Totnes,
Devon TQ9 5NP

FREE child with a paying adult with voucher
Valid from Spring Bank Holiday to end of Sept 2011

NOT TO BE USED IN CONJUNCTION WITH ANY OTHER OFFER

A superb family day out in the atmosphere of a bygone era. Explore the recreated period street and fascinating exhibitions. Unlimited tram rides are free with entry. Play areas, woodland walk and sculpture trail, shops, tea rooms, pub, restaurant and lots more.

Open: daily April to end October 10am to 5.30pm.

Directions: eight miles from M1 Junction 28, follow brown and white signs for "Tramway Museum".

FHG GUIDES, ABBEY MILL BUSINESS CENTRE, PAISLEY PA1 1TJ • www.holidayguides.com

---

The day in the country that's out of this world! With 5 major rides and loads of great live shows. See Merlin from 'Britain's Got Talent' 5 days a week. All rides and shows included in entrance fee.

Open: 10.30am - 6pm. Check for winter opening hours.

Directions: on the main A39 one mile from Clovelly.

FHG GUIDES, ABBEY MILL BUSINESS CENTRE, PAISLEY PA1 1TJ • www.holidayguides.com

---

The best day of your holiday baa none! Sheep racing, dog and duck trialling, huge indoor playground, animal barn with pets' corner and lamb bottle feeding, train and tractor rides, and much more.

Open: 10am-6pm daily April to October. From Nov-March weekends and school holidays only. Please check opening times before visiting.

Directions: two miles west of Bideford, on the A39 Atlantic Highway. Look for the big flag.

FHG GUIDES, ABBEY MILL BUSINESS CENTRE, PAISLEY PA1 1TJ • www.holidayguides.com

---

Themed exhibition, changed annually, based in a Tudor house. Collection contains items of dress for women, men and children from 17th century to 1990s, from high fashion to everyday wear.

Open: Open from Spring Bank Holiday to end September. 11am to 5pm Tuesday to Friday.

Directions: centre of town, opposite Market Square. Mini bus up High Street stops outside.

FHG GUIDES, ABBEY MILL BUSINESS CENTRE, PAISLEY PA1 1TJ • www.holidayguides.com

WOODLANDS FAMILY THEME PARK
Blackawton, Dartmouth,
Devon TQ9 7DQ
Tel: 01803 712598 • Fax: 01803 712680
e-mail: fun@woodlandspark.com
www.woodlandspark.com

*12% discount off individual admission price.
No photocopies. Valid 2nd April to 6th November*

READERS' OFFER 2011

NOT TO BE USED IN CONJUNCTION WITH ANY OTHER OFFER

COMBE MARTIN WILDLIFE & DINOSAUR PARK
Higher Leigh, Combe Martin,
North Devon EX34 0NG
Tel: 01271 882486
e-mail: info@dinosaur-park.com
www.dinosaur-park.com

One child FREE with two paying adults.

READERS' OFFER 2011

NOT TO BE USED IN CONJUNCTION WITH ANY OTHER OFFER

DORSET HEAVY HORSE FARM PARK
Edmondsham Road,
Near Verwood,
Dorset BH21 5RJ
Tel: 01202 824040
www.dorset-heavy-horse-centre.co.uk

DORSET HEAVY HORSE FARM PARK

*£1 off adult ticket, 50p off child ticket. One voucher per person.
Not valid with any other offer or family ticket/concessions*

READERS' OFFER 2011

NOT TO BE USED IN CONJUNCTION WITH ANY OTHER OFFER

ABBOTSBURY SWANNERY
New Barn Road, Abbotsbury,
Near Weymouth, Dorset DT3 4JG
Tel: 01305 871858 • Fax: 01305 871092
e-mail: info@abbotsbury-tourism.co.uk
www.abbotsburyswannery.co.uk

2 FOR 1 - one adult free with each full paying adult. Valid 19/3/11 - 30/10/11. Cannot be used in conjunction with any other offer, group rate, passport ticket or Tesco Clubcard.

READERS' OFFER 2011

NOT TO BE USED IN CONJUNCTION WITH ANY OTHER OFFER

A wide variety of rides, plus zoo and farm, makes a fantastic day out for all ages. Awesome indoor adventure centres, ball blasting arenas, mirror maze and soft play ensures wet days are fun. 16 family rides including white knuckle Swing Ship, electrifying Watercoasters, terrifying Toboggan Run, Superb Falconry Centre, Big Fun Farm, animals, tractor ride, weird and wonderful zoo creatures. An all-weather attraction.

Open: Open 2nd April to 6 November. 2011 open daily 9.30am. In winter open weekends and local school holidays.

Directions: 5 miles from Dartmouth on A3122. Follow brown tourist signs from A38.

FHG GUIDES, ABBEY MILL BUSINESS CENTRE, PAISLEY PA1 1TJ • www.holidayguides.com

---

The home of the only full size animatronic T-Rex. Explore 26 acres of stunning gardens with cascading waterfalls, exotic birds and animals. Daily sea lion shows, falconry displays, lemur encounters, 3 magnificent lions, brass rubbing centre. A great day out for all the family.

Open: 10am to 5pm (last entry 3pm). Phone or see website for opening dates.

Directions: take M5 to Junction 27. Go west along the A361 towards Barnstaple, turn right on to the A399, and then follow signs for Combe Martin and Ilfracombe.

FHG GUIDES, ABBEY MILL BUSINESS CENTRE, PAISLEY PA1 1TJ • www.holidayguides.com

---

Entertainment for all ages: fascinating daily shows, FREE wagon and tractor rides, straw fun barn, go-kart arena, gypsy wagons and Romany talks, blacksmith's workshop. Lots undercover; cafe and gift shop.

Open: 10am to 5pm Easter to end October.

Directions: On the Edmondsham Road, approx. 1½ miles from Verwood. Within easy reach of Bournemouth, Poole, Southampton, Ringwood and surrounding areas.

FHG GUIDES, ABBEY MILL BUSINESS CENTRE, PAISLEY PA1 1TJ • www.holidayguides.com

---

The only colony of mute swans in the world open to the public. Mass feeding of up to 600 swans at 12 noon and 4pm daily; baby swans hatching (end May to end June); giant swan maze to explore. Cafe and gift shop.

Open: daily 19/3/11 to 30/10/11 10am to 6pm (last admission 5pm).

Directions: off A35 at Winterborne Abbas (near Dorchester). Abbotsbury is on the B3157 between Weymouth and Bridport.

FHG GUIDES, ABBEY MILL BUSINESS CENTRE, PAISLEY PA1 1TJ • www.holidayguides.com

189

FHG READERS' OFFER 2011

KILLHOPE - THE NORTH OF ENGLAND LEAD MINING MUSEUM
Near Cowshill, Upper Weardale,
Co Durham DL13 1AR
Tel: 01388 537505 • Fax: 01388 537617
e-mail: info@killhope.org.uk
www.killhope.org.uk

2-4-1 (cheapest free) or Like-4-Like
Valid April - October 2011

NOT TO BE USED IN CONJUNCTION WITH ANY OTHER OFFER

FHG READERS' OFFER 2011

TWEDDLE CHILDREN'S ANIMAL FARM
Fillpoke Lane, Blackhall Colliery,
Co. Durham TS27 4BT
Tel: 0191 586 3311
e-mail: info@tweddlefarm.co.uk
www.tweddlefarm.co.uk

FREE bag of animal food to every paying customer.
Valid until end 2011

NOT TO BE USED IN CONJUNCTION WITH ANY OTHER OFFER

FHG READERS' OFFER 2011

COLCHESTER ZOO
Maldon Road, Stanway,
Colchester, Essex CO3 0SL
Tel: 01206 331292
e-mail: enquiries@colchester-zoo.co.uk
www.colchester-zoo.co.uk

One child FREE when accompanied by two full paying adults. Valid to end 2011 except Bank Holidays and Magic of Christmas events. Cannot be used with Colchester Zoo Gold/Platinum Card, Tesco vouchers or any other offer. CODE 909

NOT TO BE USED IN CONJUNCTION WITH ANY OTHER OFFER

FHG READERS' OFFER 2011

BARLEYLANDS FARM & CRAFT VILLAGE
Barleylands Road, Billericay,
Essex CM11 2UD
Tel: 01268 290223 • Fax: 01268 290222
e-mail: info@barleylands.co.uk
www.barleylands.co.uk

We are barleylands

FREE entry for one child with each full paying adult. Valid during 2011 - not with any other offer or on special events days.

NOT TO BE USED IN CONJUNCTION WITH ANY OTHER OFFER

Killhope is a multi-award winning Victorian Lead Mining Museum, offering a grand day out. Accompany a guide on a mine tour. Our enthusiastic team ensure you have a day to remember, finding minerals, and working as a washerboy. Woodland trails, exhibitions, Killhope shop and cafe complete a great day out.

Open: April-October 10.30am-5pm

Directions: midway between Alston and Stanhope on A689

FHG GUIDES, ABBEY MILL BUSINESS CENTRE, PAISLEY PA1 1TJ • www.holidayguides.com

---

Children's farm and petting centre. Lots of hands on with bottle feeding events and bunny cuddling etc. Indoor and outdoor play areas, indoor and outdoor go-kart tracks, crazy golf, gift shop, tea room and lots more.

Open: March to Oct: 10am-5pm daily; Nov to Feb 10am to 4pm daily. Closed Christmas, Boxing Day and New Year's Day.

Directions: A181 from A19, head towards coast; signposted from there.

FHG GUIDES, ABBEY MILL BUSINESS CENTRE, PAISLEY PA1 1TJ • www.holidayguides.com

---

One of the finest zoos in Europe due to a constant programme of development. Over 260 species to see, set in 60 acres of beautiful parkland and lakes; over 50 daily displays, an undercover soft play area, four adventure play areas, two road trains and much more.

Open: daily (closed Christmas Day) from 9.30am

Directions: follow signs from J26 off the A12 south of Colchester.

FHG GUIDES, ABBEY MILL BUSINESS CENTRE, PAISLEY PA1 1TJ • www.holidayguides.com

---

Set in over 700 acres of unspoilt Essex countryside, this former working farm is one of the county's most popular tourist attractions. The spectacular craft village and educational farm provide the perfect setting for a great day out.

Open: 7 days a week. March to October 10am-5pm; November to February 10am-4pm.

Directions: follow brown tourist signs from A127 and A12.

FHG GUIDES, ABBEY MILL BUSINESS CENTRE, PAISLEY PA1 1TJ • www.holidayguides.com

191

READERS' OFFER 2011

AVON VALLEY RAILWAY
Bitton Station, Bath Road, Bitton,
Bristol BS30 6HD
Tel: 0117 932 5538
e-mail: info@avonvalleyrailway.org
www.avonvalleyrailway.org

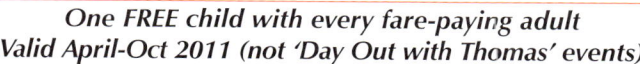

*One FREE child with every fare-paying adult
Valid April-Oct 2011 (not 'Day Out with Thomas' events)*

NOT TO BE USED IN CONJUNCTION WITH ANY OTHER OFFER

READERS' OFFER 2011

ROYAL NAVY SUBMARINE MUSEUM
Haslar Road, Gosport,
Hampshire PO12 2AS
Tel: 023 9251 0354
enquiries@submarine-museum.co.uk
www.submarine-museum.co.uk

*20% DISCOUNT on 2 tickets for visit to Museum. Valid 1/3/2011-
31/1/2012 excluding Bank Holidays and special event days. Not valid
with family, event, waterbus or any other offer. No photocopies.*

NOT TO BE USED IN CONJUNCTION WITH ANY OTHER OFFER

READERS' OFFER 2011

CIDER MUSEUM & KING OFFA DISTILLERY
21 Ryelands Street, Hereford,
Herefordshire HR4 0LW
Tel: 01432 354207
e-mail: enquiries@cidermuseum.co.uk
www.cidermuseum.co.uk

*TWO for the price of ONE admission
Valid to end December 2011*

NOT TO BE USED IN CONJUNCTION WITH ANY OTHER OFFER

READERS' OFFER 2011

DINOSAUR ISLE
Culver Parade, Sandown,
Isle of Wight PO36 8QA
Tel: 01983 404344 • Fax: 01983 407502
e-mail: dinosaur@iow.gov.uk
www.dinosaurisle.com

*One child FREE when accompanied by full paying adult.
Valid from February to December 24th 2011.*

NOT TO BE USED IN CONJUNCTION WITH ANY OTHER OFFER

The Avon Valley Railway offers a whole new experience for some, and a nostalgic memory for others.

PETS MUST BE KEPT ON LEADS AND OFF TRAIN SEATS

Open: Steam trains operate every Sunday, Easter to October, plus Bank Holidays. Tuesdays to Thurdays in school holidays, and every Wednesday in June and July.

Directions: on the A431 midway between Bristol and Bath at Bitton.

Dive into history at the Royal Navy Submarine Museum and go aboard a WWII era submarine (HMS Alliance) with a submariner to hear his stories.

Open: April-October 10am-5.30pm November-March 10am-4.30pm. Last tour one hour before closing.

Directions: exit M27 at Junction 11 and follow brown tourist signs (and anchor signs).

Learn how traditional cider and perry was made, how the fruit was harvested, milled, pressed and bottled. Walk through original champagne cider cellars, and view 18th century lead crystal cider glasses.

Open: April to October: 10am-5pm Tues-Sat. November to March 11am-3pm Tues-Sat.

Directions: off A438 Hereford to Brecon road, near Sainsbury's supermarket.

In a spectacular pterosaur-shaped building, watching over Sandown's Blue Flag beach, is Britain's first purpose-built dinosaur museum. Walk back through fossilised time and meet life-size model dinosaurs including an animated Neovenator.

Open: open all year except 24-26th December and 1st January (call for opening hours Jan/Feb).
Daily 10am-5pm (March-Oct), 10am-4pm (Nov-Feb).

Directions: on B3395 coastal road.

193

READERS' OFFER 2011

ROMNEY, HYTHE & DYMCHURCH RAILWAY
New Romney Station,
New Romney,
Kent TN28 8PL
Tel: 01797 362353
www.rhdr.org.uk

*One child FREE with every two full paying adults.
Valid until end 2011 except on special event days.*

NOT TO BE USED IN CONJUNCTION WITH ANY OTHER OFFER

READERS' OFFER 2011

CHISLEHURST CAVES
Old Hill, Chislehurst,
Kent BR7 5NL
Tel: 020 8467 3264 • Fax: 020 8295 0407
e-mail: info@chislehurstcaves.co.uk
www.chislehurstcaves.co.uk

*FREE child entry with full paying adult.
Valid until end 2011 (not Bank Holiday weekends)*

NOT TO BE USED IN CONJUNCTION WITH ANY OTHER OFFER

READERS' OFFER 2011

FARMER PARRS ANIMAL WORLD
Rossall Lane, Fleetwood,
Lancashire FY7 8JP
Tel: 01253 874389
e-mail: enquiries@farmerparrs.com
www.farmerparrs.com

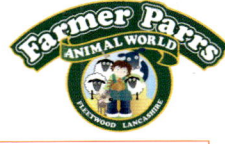

*Family ticket (2 adults + 2 children) £12.
Valid during 2011 (not for evening events.*

NOT TO BE USED IN CONJUNCTION WITH ANY OTHER OFFER

READERS' OFFER 2011

FARMER TED'S FARM PARK
Flatman's Lane, Downholland,
Ormskirk, Lancashire L39 7HW
Tel: 0151-526 0002
e-mail: farmerted@farmerteds.com
www.farmerteds.com

*TWO adults for the price of ONE when with one
child or more. Valid May-September 2011.*

NOT TO BE USED IN CONJUNCTION WITH ANY OTHER OFFER

Heritage steam miniature railway and model exhibition. 27 miles round trip following the Kent coastline. The railway runs from Hythe, Dymchurch, New Romney, Romney Sands and Dungeness.

Open: 9.45am to 6pm. Check website for details.

Miles of mystery and history beneath your feet! Grab a lantern and get ready for an amazing underground adventure. Your whole family can travel back in time as you explore this labyrinth of dark mysterious passageways. See the caves church, Druid altar and more.

Open: Wed to Sun from 10am; last tour 4pm. Open daily during local school and Bank holidays (except Christmas). Entrance by guided tour only.

Directions: A222 between A20 and A21; at Chislehurst Station turn into Station Approach; turn right at end, then right again into Caveside Close.

If ewe like animals ewe'll love Farmer Parrs. Wide selection of farm and rare breed animals, plus museum, pottery, play areas, cafe and shop. Join us down on the farm.

Open: daily all year round 10am-5pm

Directions: easy access from M55 and Blackpool. Follow the A585 towards Fleetwood/Freeport.

Family day out and fun on the farm - milking demonstrations, tractor rides, wildlife centre, indoor and outdoor adventure play areas, large restaurant. Ponies, goats, ferrets, llamas, sheep, horses and much, much more.

Open: 10am-6pm. Closed Tuesdays in low season.

Directions: on the B5195 between Ormskirk and Formby. Only 10 minutes from M58 and M57 - follow brown tourist signs.

195

NATURELAND SEAL SANCTUARY
North Parade, Skegness
Lincolnshire PE25 1DB
Tel: 01754 764345
e-mail: info@skegnessnatureland.co.uk
www.skegnessnatureland.co.uk

One child admitted FREE when accompanied by full paying adult on production of voucher. Valid to end 2011.

NOT TO BE USED IN CONJUNCTION WITH ANY OTHER OFFER

WHITEHOUSE FARM CENTRE
North Whitehouse Farm, Morpeth,
Northumberland NE61 6AW
Tel: 01670 789998 • Fax: 01670 789113
whitehousefarmcentre@tiscali.co.uk
www.whitehousefarmcentre.co.uk

*One FREE child with two paying adults
Valid until 24/12/2011 except Bank Holidays.*

NOT TO BE USED IN CONJUNCTION WITH ANY OTHER OFFER

THE HELICOPTER MUSEUM
The Heliport, Locking Moor Road,
Weston-Super-Mare BS24 8PP
Tel: 01934 635227
e-mail: helimuseum@btconnect.com
www.helicoptermuseum.co.uk

*One child FREE with two full-paying adults
Valid from April to October 2011*

NOT TO BE USED IN CONJUNCTION WITH ANY OTHER OFFER

WEDGWOOD VISITOR CENTRE
Wedgwood Drive, Barlaston,
Stoke-on-Trent, Staffordshire ST12 9ER
Tel: 01782 282986 • Fax: 01782 223063
e-mail: bookings@wwrd.com
www.wedgwoodvisitorcentre.com

*TWO for ONE offer on admission to Visitor Centre
(cheapest ticket free). Valid until end December 2011*

NOT TO BE USED IN CONJUNCTION WITH ANY OTHER OFFER

A specialised collection of animals including seals, penguins, tropical birds and butterflies (April to October), reptiles, aquarium, pets' corner etc. Known worldwide for rescuing orphaned and injured seal pups and returning almost 600 back to the wild.

Open: daily except Christmas Day, Boxing Day and New Year's Day.

Directions: north end of Skegness seafront.

Feed, hold and stroke a wide variety of animals, from traditional farm animals to a meerkat! Indoor and outdoor play areas, tractor rides, seasonal events throughout the year.

Open: Feb-Apr, Sep, Oct and Dec: Tues-Sun 10am-5pm.
May-Aug and School/Bank Holidays: daily 10am-5pm.
Jan+Nov: Sat, Sun only 10am-4pm

Directions: 3½ miles south west of Morpeth. Take A197 from A1 and follow brown tourist signs.

The world's largest helicopter collection - over 70 exhibits, includes two royal helicopters, Russian Gunship and Vietnam veterans plus many award-winning exhibits. Cafe, shop. Flights.

PETS MUST BE KEPT UNDER CONTROL

Open: Wednesday to Sunday 10am to 5.30pm. Daily during school Easter and Summer holidays and Bank Holiday Mondays. November to March: 10am to 4.30pm

Directions: Junction 21 off M5 then follow the propellor signs.

The world famous home of Wedgwood is set in 250 acres of lush parkland on the outskirts of The Potteries. Self-guided tours of the museum, craft skills demonstrations, opportunity to 'have a go'. Restaurant, boutique, shop and factory outlet on site.

Open: weekdays 9am-5pm weekends 10am-5pm

Directions: from M1 follow A50 west; from M6 follow A34, then brown tourist signs.

197

READERS' OFFER 2011

EARNLEY BUTTERFLIES & GARDENS
133 Almodington Lane, Earnley, Chichester,
West Sussex PO20 7JR
Tel: 01243 512637
e-mail: earnleygardens@msn.com
www.earnleybutterfliesandgardens.co.uk

Earnley Butterflies & Gardens

£1 per person off normal entry prices.
Valid late March to end October 2011.

NOT TO BE USED IN CONJUNCTION WITH ANY OTHER OFFER

READERS' OFFER 2011

HATTON FARM VILLAGE
Hatton Country World, Dark Lane,
Hatton, Warwickshire CV35 8XA
Tel: 01926 843411
www.hattonworld.com

One child (up to 13 years) FREE with one full paying adult (age 14+) day ticket. Not to be used in conjunction with any other offer, school/group booking or Hatton Membership; not valid Pumpkin Week or Santa's Grotto. Only one child per voucher (under-2's free). No photocopies.

 1138

NOT TO BE USED IN CONJUNCTION WITH ANY OTHER OFFER

READERS' OFFER 2011

FALCONRY UK BIRDS OF PREY CENTRE
Sion Hill Hall, Kirby Wiske
Near Thirsk, North Yorkshire YO7 4EU
Tel: 01845 587522
e-mail: mail@falconrycentre.co.uk
www.falconrycentre.co.uk

TWO for ONE on admission to Centre. Cheapest ticket free with voucher. Valid 1st March to 31st October.

NOT TO BE USED IN CONJUNCTION WITH ANY OTHER OFFER

READERS' OFFER 2011

WORLD OF JAMES HERRIOT
23 Kirkgate, Thirsk,
North Yorkshire YO7 1PL
Tel: 01845 524234
Fax: 01845 525333
www.worldofjamesherriot.org

Admit TWO for the price of ONE (one voucher per transaction only). Valid until October 2011

NOT TO BE USED IN CONJUNCTION WITH ANY OTHER OFFER

*3 attractions in 1.
Tropical butterflies, exotic animals of many types in our Noah's Ark Rescue Centre. Theme gardens with a free competition for kids.
Rejectamenta - the nostalgia museum.*

Open: 10am - 6pm daily late March to end October.

Directions: signposted from A27/A286 junction at Chichester.

FHG GUIDES, ABBEY MILL BUSINESS CENTRE, PAISLEY PA1 1TJ • www.holidayguides.com

---

Hatton Farm Village offers a wonderful mix of farmyard animals, adventure play, shows, demonstrations, and events, all set in the stunning Warwickshire countryside.

Open: daily 10am-5.30pm. Closed Christmas Day and Boxing Day.

Directions: 5 minutes from M40 (J15), A46 towards Coventry, then just off A4177 (follow brown tourist signs

FHG GUIDES, ABBEY MILL BUSINESS CENTRE, PAISLEY PA1 1TJ • www.holidayguides.com

---

*Birds of prey centre with over 60 birds including owls, hawks, falcons, kites, vultures and eagles.
3 flying displays daily.
When possible public welcome to handle birds after each display.
No dogs allowed.*

Open: 1st March to 31st October 10.30am to 5pm. Flying displays 11.30am, 1.30pm and 3.30pm daily.

Directions: on the A167 between Northallerton and the Ripon turn off. Follow brown tourist signs.

FHG GUIDES, ABBEY MILL BUSINESS CENTRE, PAISLEY PA1 1TJ • www.holidayguides.com

---

Visit James Herriot's original house recreated as it was in the 1940s. Television sets used in the series 'All Creatures Great and Small'. There is a children's interactive gallery with life-size model farm animals and three rooms dedicated to the history of veterinary medicine.

Open: daily. Easter-Oct 10am-5pm; Nov-Easter 11am to 4pm

Directions: follow signs off A1 or A19 to Thirsk, then A168, off Thirsk market place

FHG GUIDES, ABBEY MILL BUSINESS CENTRE, PAISLEY PA1 1TJ • www.holidayguides.com

MUSEUM OF RAIL TRAVEL
Ingrow Railway Centre, Near Keighley,
West Yorkshire BD21 5AX
Tel: 01535 680425
e-mail: admin@vintagecarriagestrust.org
www.vintagecarriagestrust.org

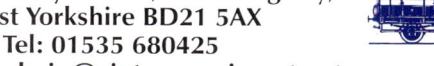

READERS' OFFER 2011

"ONE for ONE" free admission
Valid during 2011 except during special events (ring to check)

NOT TO BE USED IN CONJUNCTION WITH ANY OTHER OFFER

THE GRASSIC GIBBON CENTRE
Arbuthnott, Laurencekirk,
Aberdeenshire AB30 1PB
Tel: 01561 361668
e-mail: lgginfo@grassicgibbon.com
www.grassicgibbon.com

READERS' OFFER 2011

TWO for the price of ONE entry to exhibition (based on full adult rate only). Valid during 2011 (not groups)

NOT TO BE USED IN CONJUNCTION WITH ANY OTHER OFFER

THE ROYAL YACHT BRITANNIA
Ocean Terminal, Leith,
Edinburgh EH6 6JJ
Tel: 0131-555 5566 • Fax: 0131-555 8835
e-mail: enquiries@tryb.co.uk
wwww.royalyachtbritannia.co.uk

READERS' OFFER 2011

20% OFF admission to Britannia when presenting voucher at Visitor Centre. Valid Jan-Dec 2011 (NOT August).
Not valid with any other offer or for advance purchases. REF: 1272

NOT TO BE USED IN CONJUNCTION WITH ANY OTHER OFFER

BO'NESS & KINNEIL RAILWAY
Bo'ness Station, Union Street,
Bo'ness, West Lothian EH51 9AQ
Tel: 01506 822298
e-mail: enquiries.railway@srps.org.uk
www.srps.org.uk

READERS' OFFER 2011

FREE child train fare with one paying adult/concession. Valid April-Oct 2011. Not Days Out with Thomas or Santa Steam trains

NOT TO BE USED IN CONJUNCTION WITH ANY OTHER OFFER

A fascinating display of railway carriages and a wide range of railway items telling the story of rail travel over the years.

ALL PETS MUST BE KEPT ON LEADS

Open: daily 11am to 4pm

Directions: approximately one mile from Keighley on A629 Halifax road. Follow brown tourist signs

---

Visitor Centre dedicated to the much-loved Scottish writer Lewis Grassic Gibbon. Exhibition, cafe, gift shop. Outdoor children's play area. Disabled access throughout.

Open: daily March to October 10am to 4.30pm. Groups by appointment including evenings.

Directions: on the B967, accessible and signposted from both A90 and A92.

'Scotland's Best Visitor Attraction". Experience this floating Royal residence with a fascinating audio handset tour of five decks. Relax in the Royal Deck Tea Room.

Open: 10am - 3.30pm (last admission) Longer opening hours in summer months.

Directions: only 15 minutes from Edinburgh city centre. Tour starts at Visitor Centre on 2nd floor of Ocean Terminal.

Steam and heritage diesel passenger trains from Bo'ness to Manuel. Stop off at Birkhill for guided tours of fireclay mines. Explore the history of Scotland's railways in the Scottish Railway Exhibition. Coffee shop and souvenir shop.

Open: weekends April to October, most days in July and August. See website for dates and timetables.

Directions: in the town of Bo'ness. Leave M9 at Junction 3 or 5, then follow brown tourist signs.

MYRETON MOTOR MUSEUM
Aberlady,
East Lothian EH32 0PZ
Tel: 01875 870288
www.myretonmotormuseum.co.uk

One child FREE with each paying adult
Valid during 2011

NOT TO BE USED IN CONJUNCTION WITH ANY OTHER OFFER

SCOTLAND'S SECRET BUNKER
Crown Buildings, Troywood,
St Andrews, Fife KY16 8QH
Tel: 01333 310301 • Fax: 01333 312040
e-mail: mod@secretbunker.co.uk
www.secretbunker.co.uk

One child FREE with one full paying adult
Valid April - October 2011

NOT TO BE USED IN CONJUNCTION WITH ANY OTHER OFFER

SCOTTISH DEER CENTRE
Cupar,
Fife KY15 4NQ
Tel: 01337 810391
e-mail: info@tsdc.co.uk
www.tsdc.co.uk

One child FREE with one full paying adult on production of voucher. Not valid during December.

NOT TO BE USED IN CONJUNCTION WITH ANY OTHER OFFER

STRATHSPEY STEAM RAILWAY
Aviemore Station, Dalfaber Road,
Aviemore, Inverness-shire PH22 1PY
Tel: 01479 810725
strathtrains@strathspeyrailway.co.uk
www.strathspeyrailway.co.uk

2 FOR 1 3rd class adult return on the 1.30pm train from Broomhill to Aviemore (return departs Aviemore 2.45pm). Not available on any other trains. One free ticket per voucher. Valid 1st April to 31st Oct when trains are running.

NOT TO BE USED IN CONJUNCTION WITH ANY OTHER OFFER

On show is a large collection, from 1899, of cars, bicycles, motor cycles and commercials. There is also a large collection of period advertising, posters and enamel signs.

Open: March-Oct: open daily 10.30am to 4.30pm.
Nov-Feb: weekends 11am to 3pm or by special appointment.

Directions: off A198 near Aberlady. Two miles from A1.

FHG GUIDES, ABBEY MILL BUSINESS CENTRE, PAISLEY PA1 1TJ • www.holidayguides.com

100ft underground, Scotland's Secret Bunker is where Scotland would have been governed from, had there been a nuclear war. It is the size of two football pitches one on top of another.

Open: 10am to 5pm seven days a week, from 1st April to end October.

Directions: near St Andrews - follow brown tourist signs.

FHG GUIDES, ABBEY MILL BUSINESS CENTRE, PAISLEY PA1 1TJ • www.holidayguides.com

55-acre park with 12 species of deer from around the world. Guided tours, trailer rides, treetop walkway, children's adventure playground and picnic area. Other animals include wolves, foxes, otters and a bird of prey centre.

Open: 10am to 5pm daily except Christmas Day and New Year's Day.

Directions: A91 south of Cupar. Take J9 M90 from the north, J8 from the south.

FHG GUIDES, ABBEY MILL BUSINESS CENTRE, PAISLEY PA1 1TJ • www.holidayguides.com

Scotland's steam railway in the Highlands. Steam trains run from Aviemore to Boat of Garten and Broomhill through heather moorland and farmland by the River Spey. Recently restored ex-Caledonian Railway No.828 of 1899 pulls most trains.

Open: 9.30am to 4.30pm summer months - see website for timetable.

Directions: Platform 3 at Aviemore Station.

FHG GUIDES, ABBEY MILL BUSINESS CENTRE, PAISLEY PA1 1TJ • www.holidayguides.com

203

READERS' OFFER 2011

RHEILFFORDD TALYLLYN RAILWAY
Gorsaf Wharf Station, Tywyn,
Gwynedd LL36 9EY
Tel: 01654 710472
e-mail: enquiries@talyllyn.co.uk
www.talyllyn.co.uk

£1 OFF ticket price of full adult round trip
Not valid on special/excursion trains or Christmas services

NOT TO BE USED IN CONJUNCTION WITH ANY OTHER OFFER

READERS' OFFER 2011

INIGO JONES SLATEWORKS
Groeslon, Caernarfon,
Gwynedd LL54 7UE
Tel: 01286 830242
e-mail: slate@inigojones.co.uk
www.inigojones.co.uk

TWO for the price of ONE on self-guided tour.
Valid during 2011

NOT TO BE USED IN CONJUNCTION WITH ANY OTHER OFFER

READERS' OFFER 2011

GWILI RAILWAY
The Railway Station,
Bronwydd Arms,
Carmarthenshire SA33 6HT
Tel: 01267 238213
www.gwili-railway.co.uk

TWO FOR ONE (lowest price ticket free). Valid March-Oct 2011
except Thomas or "Special" events and/or Christmas

NOT TO BE USED IN CONJUNCTION WITH ANY OTHER OFFER

READERS' OFFER 2011

NATIONAL CYCLE COLLECTION
Automobile Palace, Temple Street,
Llandrindod Wells, Powys LD1 5DL
Tel: 01597 825531
e-mail: cycle.museum@powys.org.uk
www.cyclemuseum.org.uk

TWO for the price of ONE
Valid during 2011 except Special Event days

NOT TO BE USED IN CONJUNCTION WITH ANY OTHER OFFER

The Talyllyn Railway is a historic narrow-gauge steam railway running through the beautiful mid-Wales countryside, from Tywyn on the coast to the delightful Dolgoch Falls and wooded Nant Gwernol.	**Open:** daily from Easter to October; see website for details of timetables at other times. **Directions:** on the A493 on the Aberdyfi side of Tywyn, 300 yards from Tywyn mainline rail station and bus stops.

FHG GUIDES, ABBEY MILL BUSINESS CENTRE, PAISLEY PA1 1TJ • www.holidayguides.com

A unique, thriving, fully operational slateworks. Enter the workshops for a fascinating and inspiring insight into an ongoing era of techniques and expertise. Self-guided tours including Lettercutting and Calligraphy Exhibitions.	**Open:** seven days a week 9am-5pm. Closed Christmas/Boxing/New Year's days **Directions:** main A487 6 miles south of Caernarfon going towards Porthmadog.

FHG GUIDES, ABBEY MILL BUSINESS CENTRE, PAISLEY PA1 1TJ • www.holidayguides.com

During operating days we provide a trip back in time with a round trip on a steam-hauled locomotive in the scenic Gwili valley. Pay once and ride all day. Check website or phone for timetables.	**Open:** check website or phone for information. **Directions:** just off the A484, three miles north of Carmarthen.

FHG GUIDES, ABBEY MILL BUSINESS CENTRE, PAISLEY PA1 1TJ • www.holidayguides.com

Journey through the lanes of cycle history and see bicycles from Boneshakers and Penny Farthings up to modern Raleigh cycles. Over 250 machines on display **PETS MUST BE KEPT ON LEADS**	**Open:** 1st March to 1st November daily 10am onwards. **Directions:** brown signs to car park. Town centre attraction.

FHG GUIDES, ABBEY MILL BUSINESS CENTRE, PAISLEY PA1 1TJ • www.holidayguides.com

Index of Towns and Counties

Abergavenny, South Wales	WALES
Alford, Aberdeen, Banff & Moray	SCOTLAND
Alfriston, East Sussex	LONDON & SOUTH EAST
Alston, Cumbria	NORTH WEST
Alston, Cumbria	PET FRIENDLY PUBS
Ambleside, Cumbria	PET FRIENDLY PUBS
Ardfern, Argyll & Bute	SCOTLAND
Arlingham, Gloucestershire	SOUTH WEST
Ashbourne, Derbyshire	MIDLANDS
Axminster, Devon	SOUTH WEST
Aysgarth, North Yorkshire	YORKSHIRE
Bamford, Derbyshire	MIDLANDS
Bedale, North Yorkshire	YORKSHIRE
Berwick-upon-Tweed, Northumberland	NORTH EAST
Bideford, Devon	PET FRIENDLY PUBS
Bideford, Devon	SOUTH WEST
Bodmin, Cornwall	SOUTH WEST
Boughton Monchelsea, Kent	LONDON & SOUTH EAST
Brampton, Cumbria	NORTH WEST
Bridgwater, Somerset	SOUTH WEST
Bristol, Gloucestershire	SOUTH WEST
Broughton-in-Furness, Cumbria	NORTH WEST
Bude, Cornwall	SOUTH WEST
Bunessan, Argyll & Bute	SCOTLAND
Burford, Oxfordshire	LONDON & SOUTH EAST
Burley, Hampshire	LONDON & SOUTH EAST
Bury St Edmunds, Suffolk	EAST
Buxton, Derbyshire	MIDLANDS
Cairndow, Argyll & Bute	SCOTLAND
Chelmsford, Essex	EAST
Chester, Cheshire	NORTH WEST
Chichester, West Sussex	LONDON & SOUTH EAST
Chorley, Lancashire	NORTH WEST
Christchurch, Dorset	PET FRIENDLY PUBS
Christchurch, Dorset	SOUTH WEST
Circencester, Gloucestershire	PET FRIENDLY PUBS
Clapham, North Yorkshire	YORKSHIRE
Clitheroe, Lancashire	PET FRIENDLY PUBS
Clitheroe, Lancashire	NORTH WEST
Colchester, Essex	EAST
Coniston, Cumbria	NORTH WEST
Coventry, Warwickshire	PET FRIENDLY PUBS
Craignure, Argyll & Bute	SCOTLAND
Crieff, Perthshire	SCOTLAND
Danby, North Yorkshire	YORKSHIRE
Denbigh, North Wales	WALES
Dent, Cumbria	NORTH WEST
Dersingham, Norfolk	EAST
Dittisham, Devon	SOUTH WEST
Dolgellau, Anglesey & Gwynedd	WALES
Dorchester, Dorset	PET FRIENDLY PUBS
Dorchester, Dorset	SOUTH WEST
Dorking, Surrey	PET FRIENDLY PUBS
Dunsford, Devon	SOUTH WEST
Dunster, Somerset	SOUTH WEST
Eaton, Cheshire	NORTH WEST
Elterwater, Cumbria	NORTH WEST
Eskdale, Cumbria	NORTH WEST
Eskdale, Cumbria	PET FRIENDLY PUBS
Eton Wick, Berkshire	LONDON & SOUTH EAST
Exmoor, Devon	SOUTH WEST
Fordingbridge, Hampshire	LONDON & SOUTH EAST
Forest of Dean, Gloucestershire	SOUTH WEST
Fowey, Cornwall	SOUTH WEST
Gomshall, Surrey	LONDON & SOUTH EAST
Grassington, North Yorkshire	PET FRIENDLY PUBS
Great Ayton, North Yorkshire	YORKSHIRE
Grittleton, Wiltshire	SOUTH WEST
Happisburgh, Norfolk	EAST
Harrogate, North Yorkshire	PET FRIENDLY PUBS
Hawkshead, Cumbria	NORTH WEST
Hay-on-Wye, Powys	WALES
Hexham, Northumberland	NORTH EAST
Hindon, Wiltshire	PET FRIENDLY PUBS
Hindon, Wiltshire	SOUTH WEST
Hope Valley, Derbyshire	MIDLANDS

INDEX OF TOWNS AND COUNTIES

Huggate, East Yorkshire	YORKSHIRE
Ilfracombe, Devon	SOUTH WEST
Inverurie, Aberdeen, Banff & Moray	SCOTLAND
Keswick, Cumbria	NORTH WEST
Keswick, Cumbria	PET FRIENDLY PUBS
Kingston upon Thames, Surrey	LONDON & SOUTH EAST
Kintbury, Berkshire	LONDON & SOUTH EAST
Kirkby Lonsdale, Cumbria	NORTH WEST
Kirkby Lonsdale, Cumbria	PET FRIENDLY PUBS
Lairg, Highlands	SCOTLAND
Lamphey, Pembrokeshire	WALES
Lauder, Borders	SCOTLAND
Launceston, Cornwall	PET FRIENDLY PUBS
Launceston, Cornwall	SOUTH WEST
Leighton Buzzard, Bedfordshire	EAST
Leominster, Herefordshire	MIDLANDS
Llangollen, North Wales	WALES
Llanymynech, Powys	WALES
Loch Eck, Argyll & Bute	SCOTLAND
Longframlington, Northumberland	NORTH EAST
Longrock, Cornwall	SOUTH WEST
Lulworth Cove, Dorset	SOUTH WEST
Lynmouth, Devon	SOUTH WEST
Maidenhead, Berkshire	PET FRIENDLY PUBS
Manchester, Greater Manchester	PET FRIENDLY PUBS
Marazion, Cornwall	SOUTH WEST
Market Drayton, Shropshire	MIDLANDS
Mells, Somerset	SOUTH WEST
Milton Keynes, Buckinghamshire	LONDON & SOUTH EAST
Moffat, Dumfries & Galloway	PET FRIENDLY PUBS
Moreton-in-Marsh, Gloucestershire	SOUTH WEST
Morpeth, Northumberland	NORTH EAST
Mortehoe, Devon	SOUTH WEST
Near Sawrey, Cumbria	NORTH WEST
Newport, Pembrokeshire	WALES
Ningwood, Isle of Wight	LONDON & SOUTH EAST
Petworth, West Sussex	LONDON & SOUTH EAST
Port Isaac, Cornwall	SOUTH WEST
Rathnew, Co. Wicklow	IRELAND
Ringmer, East Sussex	LONDON & SOUTH EAST
Ringmer, West Sussex	PET FRIENDLY PUBS
Ringwood, Hampshire	PET FRIENDLY PUBS
Ross-on-Wye, Herefordshire	MIDLANDS
Rousay, Isle of Orkney	SCOTLAND
St Andrews, Fife	SCOTLAND
Salcombe, Devon	PET FRIENDLY PUBS
Salcombe, Devon	SOUTH WEST
Sandhurst, Berkshire	LONDON & SOUTH EAST
Seahouses, Northumberland	NORTH EAST
Seaview, Isle of Wight	LONDON & SOUTH EAST
Selby, North Yorkshire	PET FRIENDLY PUBS
Shalfleet, Isle of Wight	LONDON & SOUTH EAST
Skipton, North Yorkshire	YORKSHIRE
Sleat, Isle of Skye	SCOTLAND
Staveley, Cumbria	NORTH WEST
Stiffkey, Norfolk	PET FRIENDLY PUBS
Strathyre, Perthshire	SCOTLAND
Sutton Gault, Cambridgeshire	EAST
Swanage, Dorset	PET FRIENDLY PUBS
Tavistock, Devon	PET FRIENDLY PUBS
Thatcham, Berkshire	LONDON & SOUTH EAST
Thornham, Norfolk	EAST
Thurso, Highlands	SCOTLAND
Topsham, Devon	SOUTH WEST
Torpoint, Cornwall	SOUTH WEST
Troutbeck, Cumbria	PET FRIENDLY PUBS
Truro, Cornwall	SOUTH WEST
Tuckenhay, Devon	PET FRIENDLY PUBS
Ullapool, Highlands	SCOTLAND
Ulverston, Cumbria	NORTH WEST
Waddesdon, Buckinghamshire	LONDON & SOUTH EAST
Wareham, Dorset	PET FRIENDLY PUBS
Wareham, Dorset	SOUTH WEST
Wasdale, Cumbria	NORTH WEST
Windermere, Cumbria	NORTH WEST
Winterton-on-Sea, Norfolk	EAST
Yelverton, Devon	SOUTH WEST
Yeovil, Somerset	SOUTH WEST
York, North Yorkshire	YORKSHIRE

Other FHG titles for 2011

FHG Guides Ltd have been publishing an attractive range of holiday accommodation guides for over 50 years. For all kinds of holiday opportunities, they make useful gifts at any time of year. Our guides are available in most bookshops and larger newsagents but we will be happy to post you a copy direct if you have any difficulty. POST FREE for addresses in the UK. We will also post abroad but have to charge separately for post or freight.

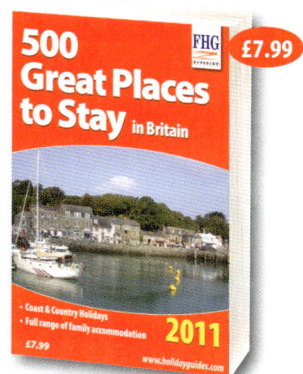

500 Great Places to Stay £7.99
in Britain
• Coast & Country Holidays
• Full range of family accommodation

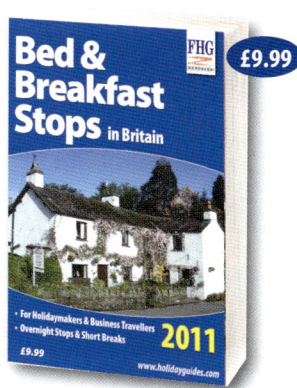

Bed & Breakfast Stops £9.99
in Britain
• For holidaymakers and business travellers
• Overnight stops and Short Breaks

The Original Pets Welcome! £9.99
• The bestselling guide to holidays for pets and their owners

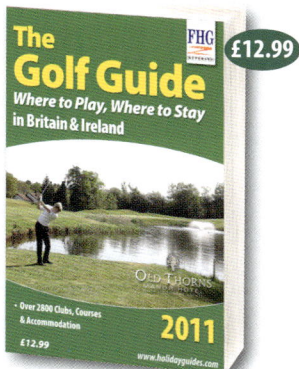

The Golf Guide £12.99
Where to Play, Where to Stay
• Approximately 2800 golf courses in Britain and Ireland plus details of convenient accommodation.

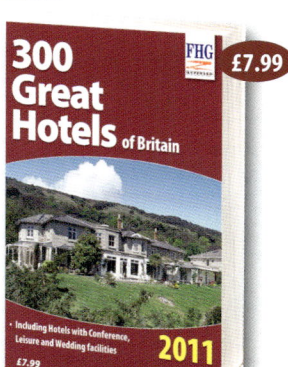

300 Great Hotels £7.99
of Britain
• Quality Hotels which offer the best of traditional hospitality and comfort.

Caravan & Camping Holidays £7.99
in Britain
• Campsites and Caravan parks
• Facilities fully listed

FHG GUIDES 2011

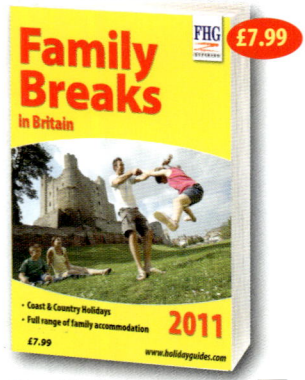 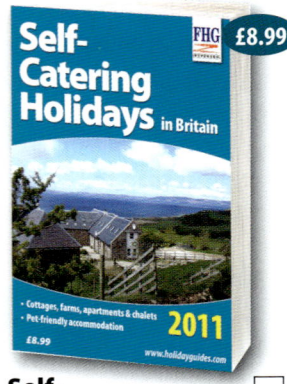 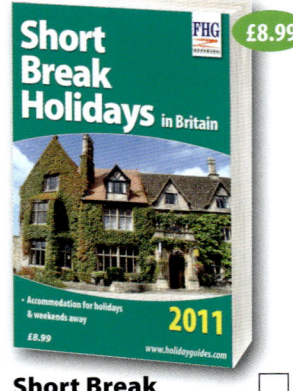

Family Breaks ☐
in Britain
• Accommodation, attractions and resorts
• Suitable for those with children and babies

Self-Catering Holidays ☐
in Britain
• Cottages, farms, apartments and chalets
• Over 400 places to stay
• Pet-Friendly accommodation

Short Break Holidays ☐
in Britain
• Accommodation for holidays and weekends away

Tick your choice above and send your order and payment to

**FHG Guides Ltd. Abbey Mill Business Centre
Seedhill, Paisley, Scotland PA1 1TJ
TEL: 0141- 887 0428 • FAX: 0141- 889 7204
e-mail: admin@fhguides.co.uk**

Deduct 10% for 2/3 titles or copies; 20% for 4 or more.

Send to: NAME ....

ADDRESS ....

....

....

POST CODE ....

I enclose Cheque/Postal Order for £ ....

SIGNATURE ....DATE ....

Please complete the following to help us improve the service we provide.
How did you find out about our guides?:

☐ Press   ☐ Magazines   ☐ TV/Radio   ☐ Family/Friend   ☐ Other